MA

D0413082

Leabharlanna Fhine Gall
MALAHIDE LIBRARY
Inv/99 : 99/1058F Price IR£7.99
Title: Letter to Veronica
Class: 920 / GUERIN

Items
belo
tele
Fi

For Graham and Cathal, your family, your friends and
colleagues and the people of Ireland bathed in tears.

14.

23.

Published 1999
by Poolbeg Press Ltd
123 Baldoyle Industrial Estate
Dublin 13, Ireland

© Michael Sheridan

The moral right of the author has been asserted.

A catalogue record for this book is available from the British Library.

ISBN 1 85371 921 8

All rights reserved. No part of this publication may be reproduced or
transmitted in any form or by any means, electronic or mechanical,
including photography, recording, or any information storage or
retrieval system, without permission in writing from the publisher. The
book is sold subject to the condition that it shall not, by way of trade or
otherwise, be lent, resold or otherwise circulated without the
publisher's prior consent in any form of binding or cover other than
that in which it is published and without a similar condition, including
this condition, being imposed on the subsequent purchaser.

Cover design by Slatter-Anderson
Cover Photo by Brian Farrell/Sunday Independent
Set by Pat Hope
Printed by Guernsey Press Ltd,
Vale, Guernsey, Channel Islands.

ACKNOWLEDGEMENTS

My heartfelt thanks to my partner Ger for her unstinting support and love during the bad days and our sons Cian and Fionn for providing light at the end of the tunnel. To my son Marty and daughter Sarah and to Maria for watching a lot of water flow under the creative bridge. To my mother Patsy and late father Martin for everything, Nigel Warren Green and Kevin Menton for risking their future in pursuit of the film project, to Catriona and Aisling for being themselves, to Clíona Ruiséil for her untiring research, to Emma O'Beirne for brilliant cross-checking, to Detective Inspector Gerry O'Carroll for opening the mine of his wisdom and experience, Paul Williams for his knowledge and company, Liz Allen for her teamwork during the Paul Ward trial. Gaye and Valerie Shortland in Poolbeg for their great editing. To the *Sunday Independent* crew Aenghus, Anne, Willie, Liam, Madelline, Aine, Sharon and Barry for tolerating my come day, go day method of work. And Brian Farrell for letting us use his dramatic photographs. I owe a debt of gratitude to Donel Geaney for providing the wherewithal to allow me write my first screen play. To Director John Mackenzie, Joan Allen, Patrick Bergin, John McDonnell, Mark Geraghty, Robert Quinn and all the cast and crew whose dedication went far beyond work to honour Veronica. To Mary Donohue for being a most understanding banker. Last but not least, Manuel and Doris di Lucia and their friends in Kilkee who tolerated, supported and subsidised my first step in film writing.

"But thy eternal summer shall not fade,
Nor lose possession of that fair thou ow'st
Nor shall Death brag thou wand'rest in his shade,
When in eternal lines to time thou grow'st.
So long as men can breathe or eyes can see
So long lives this, and this gives life to thee."

SHAKESPEARE, SONNETS

A LETTER TO VERONICA

Dear Veronica,

It seems like long ago now. But time and the tides of fortune can play tricks on the mind of man. On other occasions it could be yesterday; the image is not quite clear, like the shimmering haze of a midsummer's day, but the presence is in spirit so strong and endurable – like the memory of all great humans – that it will outlast the constant turning of the seasons.

There is not a day or hour that passes that my mind is not occupied by thoughts of you and of what might have happened had fate dealt the vital card in my hand. The card that would foresee the future and reverse the train of the past. I still cannot bear to drink the unheady liquid of reality, the fact that I will never be in your physical presence ever again.

I have experienced the passage of people I knew, as Hemingway puts it, "across the river and into the trees". People say that the older you get the easier it is to accept the death of near or loved ones. Not so. There are too many unanswered questions. Although the ritual of burial and the hope for an afterlife provide a source of consolation, there is the nagging doubt that, like the passing of Professor Isak Borg in Ingmar Bergman's *Wild Strawberries*, in the end all there is to face is – A Blank Black Screen.

It was on one of those Indian summer days on which the sky is uncommonly blue, the light crystal clear and the city looks beautiful, that we first met in a formal way. In September 1995 I had been asked to collaborate on a script dealing with the contemporary Dublin crime scene. The principal character was a cop frustrated with the system and prepared to take the crime bosses on in a confrontational way; a latter-day Lugs Brannigan and not unlike the country's leading crime reporter – you, Veronica Guerin. You were this enigmatic woman I had met on a couple of social occasions and seen in the offices of the *Sunday Independent*.

I had faced the fact that I was utterly unqualified to write a script on crime. I was very anxious to get involved in a project which dealt with contemporary issues. Too many films made by the indigenous industry are set in the distant past, located in rural areas and tend towards maudlin sentimentality. I was, if only peripherally, aware that the criminal underworld had taken a stranglehold on Dublin and a whole new generation of Bosses had emerged whose merciless attitude to life and monetary gain made the notorious criminal family of the 80s, the Dunnes, look like a bunch of handbag thieves.

I also recognised that while Ireland had made significant economic progress there was a price to pay. Greed and self-advancement are inevitable by-products of a concentration on material gain. Increasingly the professional classes were becoming involved in their own criminal activities such as embezzlement, fraud and the illegal misuse of clients' funds and laundering money for the crime barons.

A professional prisoner, whom I visited in Mountjoy, confirmed during a prison visit that he had regularly received large amounts of cash in brown-paper bags which he used to purchase a property "on behalf of a client". The client inevitably was a big figure involved in drugs or other criminal activity. The professional naturally got a cash kickback.

I realised my knowledge of the territory was too sketchy to attempt a film script, so I searched in my mind for a way to deal with this problem. I had been reading your brilliant articles on the underworld with increasing fascination, so I was determined to interest you in collaborating with me in devising a storyline that, albeit fictional, would have credibility and a foundation in truth. I rang, you responded immediately. We met in Café Java just over the bridge on Leeson Street and this would become the venue for our regular meetings over the next eight months.

When I arrived you were sitting – a coffee in one hand and a cigarette in the other – a sight which would become familiar, and characteristic of a woman who drove both her car and herself at high speed. I had not been that close to you in the office. You passed by for consultations with the editorial executives or the lawyers, and by the nature of your work those visits were infrequent.

I was greeted by a radiant smile, twinkling clear blue eyes and an affectionate kiss on the cheek which was the very opposite of what I expected from such a high-powered and dedicated woman. What one anticipates is conversation that is clipped, to the point, a certain distance, the cool attitude of the professional, one eye on the watch and the other trained at some point beyond the shoulder. It is a posture which I have come to detest; the mental uniform of the upper middle classes and higher civil servants – what Eamon Dunphy, broadcaster and journalist, refers to as "Official Ireland".

Right, you wore the suit, your blonde hair was neatly kept and the mobile phone was present but that was the only similarity with that class. I laid my cards quickly on the table. I needed an insight into the operation and characters that comprised the criminal underworld; and I wanted Veronica Guerin, whom I recognised as the expert, to help construct, as a consultant, first of all an overall picture and then collaborate in creating characters and constructing a storyline which would in pictorial form reflect the impact this criminal activity had on individuals and on society in general.

In formal terms this put you in the position of consultant but it was to become much more. You told me that your knowledge of the film medium was limited but that since you had turned down numerous book offers on the ground of lack of time this would provide another platform for the understanding of the grip the crime barons had on Dublin. Through this collaboration, you would extend the scope of your work beyond the pages of the newspaper.

I was thrilled with your reaction and immediate enthusiasm for the project, which suddenly had taken on a dimension I had never envisaged before our meeting. For two hours I listened with a mixture of trepidation, fascination and horror as you drew a detailed map of

Dublin's crime zone and provided individual profiles of the main players. Some of the material I was familiar with from your absorbing articles in the *Sunday Independent,* but the background and the additional insight you provided was staggering. It was as if, for example, the experience of watching a film like *Serpico* had been replaced by a journey in his physical presence.

I had to keep reminding myself that this was no celluloid or literary fantasy, but the tangible experience of a top crime reporter. And that reporter was you, a nervy blonde woman, of slim build and dynamic energy, chain-smoking and talking with the speed of a machinegun.

But it wasn't just the sum-total of the physical characteristics and the observations of a unique voyager among the twisting and turning corridors of Dublin's underbelly. As you talked I realised that here was a woman for whom courage and fortitude were like heart and lungs and for whom fear was never to provide the adrenalin rush that leads to running away. Veronica, you were born to fight, the concept of flight never entered your genetic dictionary.

Only once before in my life had I met someone who considered fear a minor inconvenience. My mother Patsy's brother Gus had in the 30's climbed down 600 feet of the Cliffs of Moher to retrieve the body of a young American tourist which had lodged on a ledge. On his deathbed he explained that his fear was totally subservient to bringing up the body of this crumpled little thing, like a bird with a broken neck. The fact that nobody else in the country would risk their life was immaterial. "Somebody," he told me, "had to do it."

Well, I recognised a similar attitude in your approach

to your job. Of course people thought Gus was mad to do what the experts considered impossible – those who seek to live their existence out within the safest of parameters will always wish everyone to impose the same limitations of outlook. Adventurers are regarded with a mixture of disdain and respect.

Perhaps because my eyes had been closed to what was going on in the city I love, I felt your presence at first awesome. Naturally, it is not every day you meet a real heroine in the flesh. After you had dropped me to Gardiner Street, where I was working on a video course with an inner-city group, I began to have an inkling of the quality of human endeavour it takes to be a Pádraig Pearse, Michael Collins, or Edmund Hillary. And in common with those heroes, you had a restless heart.

These are special human beings with a vision, a work method and a determination that brooks no obstacle or opposition. Integrity and honesty are natural characteristics, both qualities as rare as gold nuggets in societies driven by acquisition, greed and avarice; and all, despite inevitable human failing, motivated by a purpose which is pure, and clear. Hillary climbed Everest "because it was there", Pearse and Collins wanted a Free Ireland to take its rightful place among the nations of the earth. Veronica, you wanted to expose the activities of corrupt evil criminals so that the cancer of violence, drugs and murder could be cured.

It is arguable that life is so precious that it is a gift which should not be willingly sacrificed or indeed put at risk for a principle. But the sense of life I got from this first encounter was so strong, so vital, so harnessed that it was inconceivable that the force could ever be halted.

If there was an art to find the mind's construction in your face, it would have expressed this thought loud and clear – "Nobody is going to stop me doing what I know I have to do".

In a matter of days the Indian Summer had slipped imperceptibly into fond memory, to be replaced by an oppressive blanket of low-lying cloud and intermittent spittle descending from the grey sky.

Inside Café Java we continued our discussions and nothing could dampen your spirit, even when you began to lift the manhole at the heart of the city, to expose – like turning over a rock – a whole colony of creepy-crawlies slipping and sliding at a level of the ground beyond the reach of a snail's belly.

After you got into crime reporting in the wake of the kidnap for ransom of Bank Chief Jim Lacey in November 1993, you were amazed that there was another world in Dublin controlled by criminals who had no respect for codes, morals or life.

"I suddenly realised that here in my own backyard exists a world that no one knows anything about, with people making huge amounts of money from drugs, crime, fraud – and I felt that I and the public ought to know more about this world."

From the time you began to operate as a crime reporter you were surprised that the Dublin underworld could continue to throw up stories on a daily basis and particularly so that this underworld, this underbelly, was expanding its activities at such a rate that it was becoming a real threat to the health and stability of our society.

"This world operates under its own rules; territories are

marked out, informers are punished and extreme violence is the method of enforcement while at the same time the "crims" have no respect for each other and even less for the society that exists outside the area of their operations. The culture is different and very dangerous."

This was a territory and a *modus operandi* which no other Irish journalist had explored in such a comprehensive fashion. While I admired your fortitude and courage it struck me as a method which carried inherent risks. If the criminals operated rules which basically translated said "Fuck me and I'll fuck you twice over", where did that put a reporter who was bringing unwarranted attention on their activities?

"There are criminals who have a lot of talent and, born into another environment, would probably be highly successful and legitimate businessmen. The sophistication of their operations proves that beyond doubt. One in particular who I will discuss later fits perfectly into this category. He lives in a posh middle-class suburb and sends his kids to the best schools. Apart from what he does for a living this man is indistinguishable from his surroundings. But there are others who are truly dangerous and make me feel extremely uncomfortable. But I deal with them because, the way I work, I have to. They have no respect for anything or anybody. Maybe this is something to do with their upbringing in a bad environment which gives them a hatred of authority, particularly the law. In their view life is cheap and morals do not exist."

You don't have to be a social scientist to grasp the fact that Mountjoy prison, the rotting Victorian flagship of the penal system, is populated mainly by inhabitants of the five most deprived areas in Dublin and there are probably no more than half a dozen white-collar criminals among the 740 to 750 inmates. This is a social problem that has never been addressed and is possibly a big factor in the rise of new Irish crime barons. The new breed is more dangerous, ruthless and ambitious than anything we have witnessed before and you, Veronica, are concerned more about reporting on and exposing their territories than exploring reasons why and from where they originated. We talk about the criminal characters and you point out how aware they are of their rights and how they can exploit the inadequacies of the legal arm of Irish law.

"I don't want to sound right-wing but as far as I am concerned the justice system in this country favours the criminal and does not favour the police or you and me who try to do our jobs in a fair and balanced way. The criminals are highly organised and know exactly what is required to avoid conviction. The right to silence means they don't have to justify or explain any of their actions. There have been fourteen gangland murders over the past twelve months and not one conviction."

Your knowledge of this closed sewer was truly astonishing and I have to admit that I took to your account like a crime buff to a Patricia Cornwell novel. But then the thought kept nagging in my head: Kay Scarpetta, the heroine of the excellent American writer's novels is a fictional character, albeit backed up by meticulous research, but nonetheless a creation of the author's mind.

You, Veronica Guerin, were not. I can see your long elegant fingers bringing the cigarette to your lips. The conspiratorial expression on your defined features as you lean over the table and prepare another story by *"Listen to this . . ."* and pouring more coffee from the pot, you take in the surroundings and eye the progress of certain customers through the café. The eye of the professional.

And then the softness that transforms your face after the business is over and you talk about your pride and joy, Cathal, now six years old and heading towards Willow Park, and your husband Graham who has supported all your efforts with stoic courage. He provides the stability that enables you to pursue your objectives by a work method unknown to any other woman in this and many another land. But this is all real – you are no invention of a vicarious author hoping for fame and fortune by bringing a character into the annals of fiction.

We discuss that subject in a roundabout way. I recount my only encounter with gangland violence. I was suffering from some indefinable bug which seemed to have a deleterious effect while on a vertical level so I reclined to the horizontal at home on the couch. I looked at the pleasant August 1994 sunlight through the window and started to read one of Patricia Cornwell's books – I think it was *Body of Evidence.*

In the book there had been a murder and Kay Scarpetta had been called to the scene of the crime. The author, with typical eye for accurate detail, recounted the scene – flashing lights from the police cars, men in white forensic suits, photographers and the detectives in charge at the scene.

My absorption in this scene, which was, by virtue of the author's skill, as real as anything I had encountered on the stage or the screen, was suddenly interrupted by a newsflash on the radio. The announcer said that a prominent south-city criminal had been shot near

Ranelagh Village. At that stage it was unclear whether his injuries were fatal.

At the time I was living in Belgrave Road just about ten minutes' walk from Ranelagh Village. I dropped the book, put on a jumper, left the flat and walked down by Belgrave Square which had an atmosphere of summer tranquillity with parents playing on the swings with their young children. I turned right at the lights into Charleston Road and as I walked towards the junction with Oxford Road I was confronted by a scene which could have come straight out of Cornwell's novel. But this was real.

A motor vehicle was resting against railings directly opposite the stop sign on Oxford Road. Police cars with flashing lights were pulling up. Inside the car, the dim outline of a slumped body; the passenger window was shattered, obviously by the impact of the bullets; the windscreen was covered in blood. I felt sick. All those films and books never prepare you for the sight of a victim of an assassination.

It was the body of The General, the notorious Dublin robber baron Martin Cahill, but that did not lessen the nauseating impact. A child, perhaps one of his own, was struggling with a policeman, presumably to get nearer the shattered remains of his father. A phalanx of photographers lined the street and the flash of the bulbs had a strobe-like effect. A reporter from the *Irish Times* approached me and told me to keep my mouth shut as I did not know who was standing next to me.

There were a lot of rough-looking characters but I was in no mood to express exultation. A brutal man had been gunned down unmercifully. Did one brutal act justify another? Later that night the police would celebrate the passing of the criminal they referred to as Tango One. If they thought that the criminal fraternity had suffered a major blow they were sadly mistaken. This was, as you recognised, only the beginning of what could be described as a criminal reign of terror during which gangs and assassinations became a regular occurrence. Dublin had become a killing-field. As Yeats put it in the poem "The Second Coming":

"Things fall apart, the centre cannot hold;
Mere anarchy is loosed upon the world,
The blood-dimmed tide is loosed and everywhere
The ceremony of innocence is drowned;
The best lack all conviction while the worst
Are full of passionate intensity."

This event, we both recognised, was just the beginning.

Eventually the car was covered in a plastic sheet and the forensic boys in the white suits arrived. I didn't realise it at the time but I was present at a landmark incident which opened a flood of blood on the streets of Dublin. One way or another it made me sick to the stomach and I left the scene. It was a while before I could go back into the fiction without the real image of what I had seen intruding.

We discussed at length the ramifications of that killing and the consequences. In many ways it was a catalytic event and we agreed that a recreation of an assassination would provide a springboard for the story, from which a woman journalist would investigate the killing and come up with a story which threw new light on the claim by the IRA that it was responsible for the killing of a major Dublin criminal just before the first ceasefire was introduced in August 1994.

But of course the underworld has been a subject of curiosity for journalists and writers and film-makers since the genesis of The Mob in the depression years in America, as has the behaviour of the criminals who control and work in a territory outside the law. The real surprise was that more journalists were not taking a greater interest in the phenomenon.

Now we were sparking with ideas and the prospect of future collaboration became exciting. You protested that you did not understand the film medium; I pointed out that it did not matter a whit; what we were hoping to construct was a story that would provide an accurate reflection of the activities of the Dublin underworld and the arrogance, ruthlessness and greed of a class that had become untouchable. This I would translate into a screenplay with my then writing-partner Ronan Gallagher. So we began to piece together the jigsaw that faces every journalist, fiction writer or screenplay writer.

We did a great deal of talking about our profession, which is constantly under attack by sectional interests. Within newspapers there is another battleground of personality and, of course, ego. But we agreed that despite this the *Sunday Independent* was a stimulating place to work and you were unequivocal in your praise for the three executives you had regular dealings with: Aengus Fanning, Willie Kealy and Anne Harris.

"They give me freedom to operate," you said, *"and without that I could not do my job properly."* I commented that it might be difficult to attain the same latitude elsewhere, especially in RTE, an executive of which had

offered you a three-year contract. I proffered the opinion that the national television station tended to stifle rather than encourage talent and you replied that the question of leaving the *Sunday Independent* was something to be considered very seriously and over a long period of time.

No hasty decision would be made because basically you were happy working for those individual people – forget the organisation or the paper about which we both found plenty to be critical. You then made one of many statements that was to remain etched indelibly on the walls of my memory like the pre-historic drawings in Egyptian caves. *"I never write anything I don't believe to be the truth."* Everybody, including the criminal contacts, would lose respect for the work you were doing if you started inventing things or stories.

The example you gave was the description in an article of a boxing exhibition which was attended by a group of the criminal fraternity. One of the paper's executives handling the story thought the colour of the piece would be heightened by including a sentence saying that the hoods were quaffing champagne.

"I couldn't write this if it wasn't true, even though it was a small detail. Those guys, the criminals present, would never take me seriously again. So I phoned the hotel and found out exactly what had been served and it wasn't champagne that night."

I had rarely encountered such honesty and attention to detail in journalism.

But more surprising was the integrity – it would have been so easy to butter up the piece and who the hell would know any differently? Well, I had also got my cards marked – our project would be driven by the same principle with a

14

bit more latitude because everyone agreed that dramatic licence would not be ruled out. This was to be a feature film not a documentary.

Then and for the next eight months, I knew I was dealing with a unique woman and a journalist of very rare quality. If there were other journalists in your own area and elsewhere who were envious of your talent, they had good reason because, Veronica, you were always way ahead of the posse.

And in the future some pathetic people masquerading as journalists would betray your memory and trust, when you were in no position to reply. Excepted: your opposite number in the Sunday World, Paul Williams, with whom you competed but had nothing but respect for and whose well-researched and well-written book on The General you singled out for particular praise.

We met again in Café Java and you began to describe your journalistic relationship with your main criminal contact (John Traynor) and the no-man's-land between civilised people and the garish shadows of the underworld – awash with fiction, half truth, lies and oftentimes the plain truth which in that territory took on a different, almost obscene aspect. Because in that province where loyalty and trust have been diseased by greed and violence, self-interest reigns supreme. And yet some of the individuals have this need to unburden information to either the police or journalists, providing a mini-confessional act, the creation of a certain privilege and, of course, notoriety.

There had to be another element – these people had, apart from the occasional magazine piece, never talked to a journalist, much less a female reporter, on a regular basis before. I wondered, apart from the unburdening or confessional aspect, why they should talk directly to a journalist who was not engaging in a public relations exercise? There had to be some element of persuasion involved.

"I suppose there is that element in being able to get a contact or criminal to relax and talk as if he was unaware of the fact that he was giving information to a journalist. If someone came by, it would be just like we are talking – nobody would know the difference – just sitting here having an informal chat. But with a criminal nothing is informal, everything is calculated like a chess game. There has to be a certain element of trust, however primitive. That's why you don't write shite like they were quaffing champagne because they'd say – if she gets that wrong – what about the trust? And sometimes some guy will, halfway through a conversation, stop and say 'I don't know why the fuck I'm talking to you. Why the hell should I trust you?' At those moments, you sit tight and speak and listen for a long time more than if you were talking to a contact. As in any other branch of journalism you have to hold out because the next time you call round he could shut the door in your face."

Over a period of time I would get to understand this extraordinary work method, the skill, the patience and the persistence in the face of dangerous people who thought nothing of inflicting violence on others – you included. But then it struck me as exciting, conspiratorial and giving the adrenalin pump that only living on the edge can offer. It shows how the uninitiated can easily be blinded. I had never actually sat opposite a dangerous criminal. Then I could just imagine along the lines of what I experienced through movies. One thing for sure, I had not the bottle for this business. We mentioned some of the hard men of the crime scene who would fall under the category of psycho, for whom violent acts had no greater significance than swallowing a pint.

"There are criminals I deal with who scare me – that's all part of it – but with those who could be regarded as psychos the feeling is different. They never lose a sense of themselves, or forget who they are talking to and never ever let their defences down. But like our side of the fence, there are all kinds of individuals and you have to learn to distinguish between them, because there is what is termed an 'ordinary decent criminal' who has grown up in his profession and has a wife and kids at home whom he genuinely loves. But there are also those who don't understand the word 'trust' and would sell their mother to get what they want."

John Traynor was an individual who never really grew up, an overgrown bulk of a man who had seen too many Mafia films and who, approaching his half-century was married with children but still chasing young skirts and driving flash racing cars in Mondello. Pathetic sure, but useful for a while and like all those who walk in the constant shadow of death, dangerous.

I know you, being an intelligent woman, were aware of all those things and you told me that you were fascinated by the Machiavellian machinations of the underworld revealed on many occasions by your informant-in-chief, for whom you alternately displayed affection, contempt and in the latter stages an attitude bordering on hatred for which you had good reason. Traynor, you explained, was a con man nicknamed "The Coach" with a prison record for house-breaking, fraud, handling firearms and handling stolen goods.

Like all criminals he could be a staunch ally on one hand

or a dangerous adversary on the other. Traynor proved to be both, while he was giving information to journalists and police, he was also breaking those confidences to the Godfathers. But he was useful because of his connections with all the major crime figures, including the late Martin Cahill, "The General". Traynor, like all informers, was a valuable source even if he was a loudmouth and a boastful braggart.

There is little doubt that as a perennial womaniser he found you attractive, a compliment that was not returned. You considered that his only attraction to undiscerning women was a fat wallet and apparently lavish lifestyle. He clearly relished the act of passing information to a woman as opposed to a policeman.

But I can confirm to those sewer rats of journalism, who in cowardly innuendos suggested that there might have been something going on between you and him, that nothing could be further from the truth. You would roar with laughter in that explosive beam that lit up Café Java at the thought.

Forgive me, Veronica, I digress and feel utterly depressed by the fact that I can no longer sit opposite you at the café table. So little is my loss compared to others, but I am sure that anyone who crossed your path would be similarly touched.

Back to Traynor, who despite his flamboyance, you pointed out, knew the dangers of the game he was playing which in its essence was a Russian roulette of betrayal. But despite impressions to the contrary, he was bothered by the role he was playing and fearful like all cowards. So he drank heavily and chain-smoked; not the habits of a man who was at ease with himself.

Someday, he knew all those broken confidences would catch up with him, but in the interim he was prepared to sacrifice anyone – including Veronica Guerin – to save his own thick skin. It took you some time to realise this side of Traynor's nature because, despite his track record of working closely with The General on a number of top criminal jobs, he had provided some great information, including the extraordinary family arrangements of The General who had a relationship and children by his wife's sister, Tina.

And Traynor, despite his bullshit and bragging, had a certain rough charm and you were grateful to him for being such a good source of great crime stories, including damning information on other crime figures. Around this time there were a lot of gangland murders and Traynor boasted that he knew who had pulled the trigger on who and why.

While you could not publish the names of the perpetrators for legal reasons, this information provided fascinating and invaluable background on the Dublin criminal underworld, which since the assassination of The General, Martin Cahill, the then crime king, in August 1994, had become a bloody battleground.

Most of the murders remained unsolved; the police and society seemed to be indifferent to the increasing violence. If the scum were killing the scum, then that was alright. You considered that to be a highly dangerous and immoral attitude on the part of the authorities who were in effect condoning the violence by not pursuing the perpetrators with the diligence applied to the murder of ordinary respectable citizens.

What you identified was the fact that the killers knew

that they were in no danger of being punished and that this would encourage an attitude of arrogance and untouchability among the godfathers who ordered the hits. And the arrogance was becoming increasingly obvious in the manner of the hits. Many were being carried out in broad daylight in public places. The builder Paddy Shanahan was shot outside a gym in Drimnagh; John Reddan, another underworld figure was shot in the Blue Lion pub in central Dublin and drugdealer Gerald Lee was gunned down at 7am while celebrating his birthday at an all-night party. What you identified and underlined was that police inaction in gangland slayings was not only morally wrong on the basis that a life is a life, but actively promoted violence by allowing the crimes to go unpunished.

"It's when nobody seems to care that it really bothers me and the reason that they don't care is most worrying. John Reddan was gunned down in the Blue Lion at 6 o'clock on a Monday night. This guy walks into the bar, goes to the toilet and then comes back, no disguise, just pulls his hat down a bit over his eyes, pulls out a gun, calmly blows Reddan's brains all over the bar and walks slowly out of the pub. This murder makes a small item on the Monday night news, a little bit in the Tuesday papers and nothing else. Why aren't the crime reporters writing about it? Because Reddan was just a lowly criminal and the police and the papers think he is expendable because he comes from the other side. The scum are killing each other. Good – one less – that is the attitude and this is a highly dangerous view because eventually these killers will engender an attitude, among the public, of complacency about violence and the criminals will get more arrogant and more dangerous because they know that they can kill and get away

*with it. And I am worried about the media attitude which
relegates these assassinations to the small-item category. The
criminal attitude is compounded – 'He had it coming to him'
– and the police or the press aren't going to bother. This gives
the murderers an even greater comfort – they can get on with
the job without fear of retribution."*

Today I shudder at the prescience of your words
because of the implications for yourself. And how much
more meaning they assume with the benefit of hindsight.
How blind it seems the rest of us were at the time. I know
people listened to you but like all prophets, your
statements were taken on board, neither too wisely nor
too well. And with the strange logic with which life deals
out the cards, the man who was suspected by police of
being involved in the shooting of John Reddan and
Paddy Shanahan is the one named by police as being
suspected of shooting you. His name is Eugene Holland.

Many a time you repeated this view to me and having
been present shortly after The General was assassinated
and feeling revulsion, I entirely agreed. The cancer of
violence had spread like wildfire through Dublin and
nobody but Veronica Guerin seemed to be doing
anything about it. It was only a matter of time until the
godfathers would start shooting anyone who got in their
way, outside their own territory.

People who think that you were obsessive only have to
see the cool logic in your motivation with regard to murder
and violence to consider you as naive. Not once did I think
of you as obsessive or naive. Determined, focused, committed
to the point of stubbornness. Driven, yes. Perhaps at the
start, too trusting of your chief criminal contact.

But as far as some underworld figures were concerned,

John Traynor's tongue was far too loose, particularly in relation to the exclusive stories about Martin Cahill's private life and there was growing unease about the exposés of crime figures and their activities. The fact that their identities were hidden behind nicknames such as The Coach, The Fixer, The Boxer, The Monk, did not really matter. By international standards, Dublin is a village and these people were becoming known to a much larger audience than the immediate communities in which they lived and operated.

You talk about this with a sense of excitement as opposed to fear, something which I never truly understand. Have you no fear? *"Of course,"* you reply. *"I'll tell you about that later."* But it all relates to what we are talking about – Traynor. I admit that I am only getting my head around all this – you are used to operating in this shadowy land and dealing with its faceless inhabitants.

Here we have this middle-aged con man who is known to take on mistresses and consort with prostitutes and mix with killers and live a flamboyant life straight out of *Goodfellas*. How could you talk to such a person, much less develop a professional relationship? It's much worse than that you say, much worse. *"Listen,"* and I do with a mixture of excitement, fascination and dread to the chilling account of your first shooting.

Now, as I am writing, I am overcome with a crushing feeling of loss, and I think of Graham and Cathal and their courage and fortitude and how indulgent my emotion is by comparison to theirs. But then I think you are alive in my thoughts every single day, and so it must be for your loved ones, and often I am consoled by a memory that created much mirth between us.

We had arranged to meet in Café Java at 11am. I got there at about 10.30; as our usual table was occupied, I moved to the other end of the room, just behind the wall angle. I read the papers and when you did not appear on time I didn't worry – a busy woman has a dispensation when it comes to time-keeping. But when half past midday came, I thought fuck this, she has forgotten, never happened before, but there is always once.

I returned to the *Sunday Independent* office and as I walked in, news editor Willie Kealy called me over. "I have a message from Veronica." Yeah? "This will be the last time you ever fuckin stand me up." But I was in Café Java until 12.30, I protested. "Well, so was she. That's rich," he said removing his glasses. "The country's top investigative reporter and one of our high-profile writers couldn't even find each other in a small café."

We had in fact been sitting back to back, both behind the wall angle. We had a good laugh at the next meeting. Needless to say we never missed each other again.

Throughout the dark days of the winter of 1995, we continued our serpentine walk through the murky labyrinth of the Dublin crime underworld and one by one you gave me profiles of the major players who had two things in common: fabulous wealth and total ruthlessness.

I questioned you at length about the dangers posed directly to a crime reporter who investigates in such a direct and unequivocal manner the dirty deeds of the Dublin Godfathers and the threats, shootings and beating you had been subjected to in the course of your investigations. As this conversation expanded over several meetings – you were clearly aware of the danger to your being; you had an intimate experience and understanding of fear; you did not underestimate the intentions of the criminals who found your work more and more intrusive but you were not going to be deflected from your work of exposing them by the knowledge of what they were capable of doing.

If the people you worked with in the *Sunday Independent,* or your police contacts, or your family, or me, argued against this course of action, you would listen politely and reply logically that you had an important job to do – law and order had broken down, the ordinary citizens of this country and city were under threat, the criminals were reaping vast rewards during the reign of terror, somebody had to do the job of exposing their evil ways and it was your duty to carry on and not give in to intimidation. So we discussed in detail the facts and effects of a variety of violent acts against you and the less obvious reasons behind them.

There were a number of shots put through the window of your home. And while this incident was being investigated by the police, they found evidence in the shape of unspent bullets in the garden, evidence of a previous botched attempt. Finally there was the actual shooting when a gunman burst into your home. Your first accounts of those incidents will ring clear in my mind forever and anyone who speculates that the badge of courage can be worn without fear will be sadly disappointed.

Listening to you talking, I tried like any of your myriad admirers to put myself in your place and grasp the true significance of your reaction to those horrifying events. I discovered very quickly, by measuring my cowardice against your courage and determination, what an extraordinary woman, what a unique human being I was dealing with and that by comparison, I was a lily-livered coward, a status that would be shared by the vast majority of the Irish population.

When I ventured to communicate this you told me to "go and shite" and the walls of Café Java resounded with our laughter – Veronica Guerin was never going to be cast in the role of a modern-day Joan of Arc. She suffered for her cause but never once did you see yourself as a martyr because you were an extraordinary woman but at the same time self-effacing. Although you were excited about our film project, essentially you were not a cinema-goer but simply saw the possibilities of expanding your work in another medium.

There is a line that I will never forget from John Herr's *Dispatches* – the brilliant account of his coverage of the Vietnam war. During the description of a bloody battle, it kept going through his mind – "It's not like the movies". You never saw yourself as a Serpico or fell into the fantasy that most of us would indulge and make falsehood of our intentions. You lived it – we dreamt it.

You relived the real shooting and its detail raised the hairs on the back of my neck. The memory is permeated by the present as is every memory – the slant of a sunlight shaft through the window as I write brings me back to a similar light as the dark days of winter gave way to the first awakening of spring's welcome arrival. Not so very long ago you were so alive, so intense and so radiant, even as you described those revolting deeds and your reaction.

I experience a deep pang of loss. I can see you as if you were sitting opposite this table or as Graham and Cathal would and your extended family in their own houses. Since those heady days there is a screaming gaping hole in all our lives. These digressions seem unwarranted, but the constant reminders of loss are what we all gained from your life.

It was a dark night on the second last day of January 1995 around tea-time, you told me. The previous Sunday you had written an article on another major criminal, The Monk, whom you named as the prime suspect in the Brinks Allied robbery, which netted somewhere between £2m and £4m and the probable leader of two other major robberies which netted millions through meticulously planned operations carried out with great ingenuity and audacity. You had, in your usual fashion, confronted this man whom you recognised as the single most dangerous crime godfather in the country, who had assumed this position after the assassination of Martin Cahill.

You had approached this man with great trepidation as a result of information you had received in relation to his control of his operations and ruthlessness in dealing with anyone who had crossed his path. And yet you found something different and fascinating about a man who earned his nickname from his abstemious appetites for food, drink and the high living so characteristic of the other Dublin godfathers who lived to indulge the fruits of their labours in all sorts of degenerate behaviour.

This man was something apart, in another league, and the first thing that struck you was his eyes which were as cold as ice and his stare which was frightening. He said that he did not want anything written about him, why couldn't you write about politicians and crooked professionals, he was just a family man who wanted to be left alone.

He denied any links with drug-dealing or the IRA. But

he was questioned by the Provos in the wake of the loyalists' aborted attempt to bomb the Widow Scallan's pub during a Sinn Féin fund-raising function. He claimed that other criminals were trying to set him up by parking a car, used in the loyalist operation, on his territory, in the north inner city the night before. Therein was the kernel of a fascinating story which you unfolded in the following sessions and which I will come back to.

You made it clear that there was nothing comfortable about confronting this dark and extremely dangerous horse of the Irish criminal world. But you were determined to do it and your article was not only uncompromising but revealed highly interesting facts about the Monk, including his ownership of extensive property and the fact that he had availed of tax amnesty to declare £200,000 of previously undeclared income, a sum on which he paid £30,000.

This story was a typical Veronica Guerin coup, a combination of well-sourced, meticulously researched fact and the hard-nosed confrontational approach to the criminals which you pioneered.

Dangerous, yes of course, but you never believed that anything you wrote, however near the edge, or anything any other journalist wrote could lead to anyone being shot.

But on the evening of January 30, 1995 the crime bosses showed just how far they were prepared to go to prevent their activities being investigated. It was at that time the most frightening moment of your life. You answered a knock on the door, almost absent-mindedly, and suddenly you were confronted by a gunman disguised by a motorcycle helmet who entered and shut the door behind him. All you could see was the gun barrel, in those chilling seconds magnified to the size of a cannon, pointed at your head. Instinctively you fell to the floor, screaming and curling into the foetal position. The gun was lowered from your head and a moment later you felt a stinging sensation in your thigh. After he left, you were able to drag yourself to the phone and ring for help.

In my mind, this account was like a slow-motion sequence from a film with the gun barrel in close-up, about to explode and then lowered. What I didn't appreciate was the naked terror of the situation; the raw fear was beyond me then but later I would become somewhat acquainted with the feelings that you must have encountered on a regular basis.

"No journalist believes he or she will ever be shot. Never, even in the most frightening moments of my investigations into Dublin's organised crime gangs, did I think it might happen to me. Until the moment I answered the door to a gunman, I never believed my work might lead to my murder. It sounds dramatic but for a few chilling seconds when I looked at the gun pointed directly at me, I truly believed I was about to die.

I do not consider myself a brave woman. But that event at the time was terrifying, the most frightening of my life, the most frightening moment I hope I shall ever have to face again. When I think back it does not seem as bad – it takes on the meaning of a warning rather than a genuine attempt on my life."

You were talking at some time removed from the event, so perhaps the immediate terror you had experienced had abated, just as grief does after the loss of a loved one. You described the shooting as if you were the centre of a drama, somewhat enhanced in effect by remembrance. But I could not disguise my horror – the writer like the actor gets to the centre of things by reliving the incident. All I could think of was that helmeted gunman. By then, helmet motorcycle killers had become the Horsemen Of The Apocalypse in Dublin. And the gun . . . I placed myself in your shoes and shivered.

The bullet had shaved your artery, you were very lucky to be alive. Did the gunman intend to kill you? No – you said it was a warning; a warning, I remarked, that so nearly went disastrously wrong.

"Of course the cops will consider the possibility that this was a genuine attempt to kill me – the forensics suggest that the first bullet jammed. There is even a crazy theory that I set it all up as a publicity stunt to get a higher profile as a crime reporter. It is so laughable that it is not worth thinking about although I wouldn't mind getting my hands on whoever circulated that one. It is just something about the whole body language of the gunman, there was an awkwardness, a sort of lack of intent. The gun was old hat. There have been enough hits in Dublin to know if they intended to kill me, it could have been easily arranged with a professional gun for hire. A modern weapon would have blown half my leg away. No, I am sure it was intended as a warning – 'Back off – you are getting too close to the bone'."

And I suppose for most people that would be enough. Yes, but nonetheless a warning that you never believed would happen to you, but then nobody believes it will happen to them – like cancer or a heart attack – things that happen to other people. The General didn't think that he would end up on the wrong side of five bullets, although if the story was to be known he had every reason to fear such an eventuality.

I recall the night they shot you. Some of our colleagues had arrived in a restaurant in Sandycove for a belated *Sunday Independent* Christmas party, all in good spirits, looking forward to a good night. And then before the party had started a phone call came – Veronica has been shot at her home. I can clearly remember the shock and the disbelief. Who would do such a thing, who would want to shoot a woman in her own home, possibly in front of her husband and child? Only once in the 25 years of the northern conflict had a journalist been shot. *The Sunday World's* Northern Editor, Jim Campbell, had survived a loyalist assassination attempt. They could have come back – they didn't.

We discussed the implications for you and for Graham and Cathal. There was a family conference and you decided to continue, with Graham's blessing. What's the point of giving into them, you argued, that's just what they want. Then they can just continue doing it to everybody else. So you carried on.

Well, I wouldn't. In my time with you later I gathered some inkling of the utter ruthlessness of the Dublin criminal class who frankly scared the shit out of me and I came to understand the atmosphere of fear and loathing in which you worked on a daily basis. So I and ninety-nine percent of others would have backed down.

"I suppose hindsight is a great thing but how many of us have used this phrase – 'If I knew then what I know now' – but that's life. If anyone had told me when I was embarking on a career as a crime reporter what I was going to encounter,

I would have taken up the gardening column. But since you don't know what is around the corner you keep going on down the road. All my life I was never easily intimidated and I am certainly not going to start now. Of course I considered whether it was worth all this violence and upset. But I concluded that it would be worse for me and for journalism if I gave up. I was aware from Garda sources that four months before the shooting I was under threat from a north-inner-city criminal for linking him to the assassination of Martin Cahill in August 1994. I knew that was a dangerous story when I wrote it because it went against the accepted theory that it was the IRA alone who carried out the hit, and exposed another dimension of the Dublin underworld. A few weeks after the General was shot I also had a great story about his personal relationships with his wife and her sister. I would have been a fool not to realise that this would cause resentment and anger among both the Cahill family and the gang. But what are you to do? Anticipate a reaction and not write the story?"

There are people who would interpret this as almost deliberately putting yourself into the firing line by incurring the wrath of two major Dublin criminal gangs and conclude that for your own good the paper should put a leash on you. But here were two great stories which no journalist worth their salt could have passed over. And they might easily forget that Woodward and Bernstein covered the break-in at Watergate and the subsequent events at the risk of their lives. How often were they warned about the danger by their source, Deep Throat? And yet Ben Bradlee did not put a leash on the reporters while story after story in *The Washington Post* tore down the fabric of the Nixon administration. But they didn't get shot and you did. So why not take a low profile, even for a while?

"I'd lose so much if I gave in to them and that would mean they won and there is no way the criminal bosses should be allowed to win. I really believe that me and my colleagues' continued exposure of these guys is actually contributing to their demise – they'll always be here because they are part of this culture now and that's an awful thing. But I feel we are doing something useful. So I've got to carry on."

I find this courage astounding and the logic of your motivation so clear and consistent. One of your original arguments was that the value of life in our capital had been diminished by the constant killing. If you were being warned off your path of restoring this value and at the same time exposing the perpetrators of death on the streets and through drugs in the housing projects, there was no way you were going to be intimidated – in the words of the Tom Petty song – *"I won't back down and I'll stand my ground"*.

But I needed you to go over the shooting in more detail, as if you were living through it again, and not just recalling with the immunising effect of the past. This time the account was more graphic, more terrifying and gave the proper value to the courage needed to carry on and not be freaked by what had happened that dark January evening.

The most searing image again, second time around, was the gun –

"I just saw the gun, nothing else, and the first thought that went through my head is that he means business. I don't know why but instinctively I went into the foetal position and he put the gun to my head and I began to roar – it wasn't a scream – and then I felt the gun on my thigh. I didn't hear the

shot but I felt a stinging sensation in my thigh. I heard his footstep running away, and then it sank in. And I just said, Jesus, I've been shot."

How anybody could have continued to work on after such a hideous experience is beyond me, because that account is so graphic that I can feel the gun against my head as anyone reading this could.

The publicity surrounding the shooting made you into a national figure, but few including myself at that time realised the significance of your decision to carry on the battle against the crime bosses. What I have to remind myself is that it was made against a backdrop in which law and order was an impotent force against the godfathers. The Government was gripped by apathy, the politicians didn't give a fuck and many of the police crime fighters recognised a lack of will on their superiors' part in doing anything about the emergence of half a dozen homegrown versions of the infamous New York Mafia boss, John Gotti. And his Irish counterparts were adopting the same killing policy as the Cosa Nostra. It was this vacuum, however scary, that you filled. People scorn in retrospect the comparison with the Untouchables but that precisely described the status of the Dublin crime bosses who were involved almost daily in violence that echoed that mob gang in Al Capone's Chicago. The one difference was that we didn't have Eliot Ness, we had Veronica Guerin, who as a lone investigative reporter was far more exposed than the great detective ever was.

Of course you got Garda protection after the shooting, but in time you recognised that you could not maintain your criminal contacts if you were being tailed by the police. It was a matter of balance; one thing that

Veronica was not going to do was rely on police sources alone, like a lot of her rivals in crime reporting. You told me that it was stifling.

"I mean you can do fuck all if you are trying to be a crime reporter and you have two guards walking around with you. Besides the crims would never talk to you if they knew that there was a Garda car around the corner."

While we talked out and through serious issues, you always maintained a great sense of humour, the saving grace of all great and earnest people, and expressed affection for your colleagues and rivals and love for your family. There was never any indication in all the time we spent in Café Java and on the phone that you allowed your single-mindedness and dedication get in the way of your compassion and above all the human touch.

Today I arranged to meet a friend in "our café". I walked through the small park in Ranelagh and watched the blooming daffodils dance gently in the breeze, the water of the pond transformed into a thousand shimmering, sparkling jewels by the spring sunlight. People passed me with a bounce in their step. I remember last year and I am enveloped in a cloud of depression. Twelve months ago you were one of those daffodils, the sparkling jewels were your eyes, the sunlight the radiance of your smile. I know I am not the only one beset by such thoughts – all those close to Veronica Guerin are similarly haunted.

I walk out through the park gates. "What the fuck is this life all about?" runs through my mind like a constantly thrusting sabre. I am not comforted by the usual sources of consolation – you have achieved so much, I know, a shining beacon in a black cesspit – but you never thought of yourself as a martyr and neither did I. We discussed all this, worked it out. Which one of us miscalculated? All I really know is that I sit at the table in Café Java and the space you once occupied is empty. Don't worry, you would say, but the emptiness is screaming at me, mocking me, goading me. As I walk back through the park, I watch daffodils full of vigour, colour, beauty. This time next year there will be daffodils, different daffodils, but nonetheless I can experience their beauty; next year that chair will be empty and the year after. If that is natural, if that is fair, if that is just, find me another world to live in. Fuck that.

I flashback in time. You described your determination, after you had recovered from the operation, to find the man who had ordered the shooting, because it was no maverick job. One of the bosses was trying to shut you up and you wanted to know who. This was either an exraordinarily clever or foolish course of action.

"I really wanted to know who had ordered the shooting. I wanted to confront the person face to face. It sickened me that someone I had sat down and talked with had been planning this all along and I felt a deep sense of betrayal. I didn't want to sit down with that person ever again without knowing because of course it put me at a disadvantage."

On the way to the home of the boss, who at the time fitted the profile of a prime suspect, Graham had to stop the car twice while you got sick. I have experienced fear that has paralysed me, made me want to pee in my trousers and get slightly breathless, but never fear that made me physically ill.

That demonstrated just how much bravery it took to pursue your course of action. As it turned out, he was not at home and although you did not know it at the time you were barking up the wrong tree. The Monk might be a cold-blooded, ruthless criminal, but what marked him out from the other crime bosses was the fact that in his particular line of business, armed robbery at the highest level, he had to have more than the average amount of brain cells.

We discussed the Monk at length as we did the other major criminal figures who dominated Dublin gangland. This man was different from the rest. This one did not hunt with the pack.

"Within the underworld there is what is commonly described as honour among thieves. I don't know if that is honour at all or just the fact that if one slags off or pulls a fast one on another they will end up with a bullet in the head. One thing is for sure, the crims are not all the same no more than journalists are. I always thought the Monk was unique. He refused to discuss the business of other criminals. 'I'll answer any questions you ask about me, but if you are gonna ask about other criminals I'm not going to talk,' he said."

We talked about the reason for this, apart from the caution that the Monk (who lived a quiet life in a Northside up-market housing estate with his wife and five kids) would exercise. You had little doubt that the Monk was not averse to the common gangland method of retribution but when we considered, with information from a police contact, that his mentor and business partner Paddy Shanahan had been assassinated we saw him in a different light. Paranoia came with the spate of gangland executions. Twice a week criminal hardman Shanahan visited a health club in Drimnagh for karate and fitness classes. He was well-built, prone to violent outbursts and was feared among the criminal classes. If

Paddy Shanahan told someone to "fuck off", he was well advised to get out of sight. The Monk looked up to Shanahan who was almost 20 years his senior and had invested money in some of his mentor's building projects. It was on one of these, an apartment block on Buckingham Street in the north inner city, that Shanahan ran into trouble. As happens with building, there was an inevitable delay and an investor who had put up £500,000 wanted his money back. When Shanahan couldn't pay up he offered to give the investor five apartments, but as property was not so buoyant in 1994 the investor refused the offer. In October of that year, Shanahan was on the way to carrying out his usual exercise routine when he was confronted by a gunman outside the Drimnagh Gym and shot once, the bullet entering just below the right eye. Shanahan died. There is no doubt among police sources that this investor – a well-known Dublin criminal – was responsible for Shanahan's death. And they believe that he used a hired assassin.

A police contact who interviewed the Monk in the wake of the murder found the gang boss a "very presentable and articulate young man". But also very distressed by the killing of his mentor. "Nowadays any punk," he told the detective, "can pull up on a motorcycle and blow you away." The gang boss was summing up a sign of the times; no one, including him, was safe from the gunmen. Before the detective left, the Monk asked his advice about security. "Retire," was the policeman's reply. He knew that the gang bosses, particularly those involved in drug-running had got more powerful and more ruthless and would stop at nothing to protect their new-found wealth and power. Hence the Monk's reticence to talk about other criminals, even off the record.

We returned to the source of the Monk's wealth. Armed robbery and property investment. But armed robbery was much more risky in terms of surveillance and entrapment than drug-dealing where the potential long-term profit was even bigger. Even investing the proceeds of robbery in drugs would bring bigger and quicker dividends for the investor. You were adamant that the Monk was not involved in drugs at any level.

"The reason I accept the Monk is not involved in drugs is because it is part of his own creed – the anti-drugs culture. He was born and bred in the north inner city which has been devastated by heroin for the past fifteen years. He was part of a young teenage crime gang known as the Bugsy Malones and after serving a prison sentence he came out at sixteen to find that all his pals were into the drug culture. His time inside probably kept him away from drugs and when he saw the effects he vowed to keep away from them. When I spoke to him he was genuinely emotional because most of the original Bugsy Malones were either dead or dying from drugs-related illnesses like over-dosing and AIDS and some of his own relatives were caught in the web. He is unequivocal about the subject – "My community know that I don't do drugs. I don't do them, I don't sell them and I don't finance them, end of story."

I wondered how easy it was to accept the word of a criminal, however credible and however persuasive. You told me that you had spoken to the guards, to the highest level community workers, welfare officers and drug counsellors and the consensus of opinion was that if anything, the Monk would dissuade young people from taking drugs. What would further confirm his contention was the fact that he is very much a family man and takes a great interest in his own children, sparing no expense for their education. Drug barons, by contrast, did not seem to care about their children and actively involved them in the culture to the extent that many of them became addicts as young as thirteen years of age. Now while you had clearly established a rapport with the Monk, you were in no way interested in painting him as a saint, as the article on the Brink's Allied robbery published the day before you were shot proved in abundance, as did the lengths you were prepared to go to check out in his own inner city community, before accepting his word on the drugs issue. So you were not about to act as his public relations agent and you were fully aware of the tangled web of agendas in the underworld in which you could easily be manipulated or used. But you recognised that the Monk was a class apart.

The other bosses – the Coach, the Warehouseman, the Tosser, the Boxer, were characterised by cunning and a liking for ostentatious lifestyles, wine, women, song and lots of exotic foreign holidays. The Monk lived for his family with whom he holidayed. His limited indulgences were attending world championship fights involving Steve Collins and supporting Manchester United at matches in England, a passion which ironically you shared, in one of many contradictions – Veronica Guerin and the number one criminal in Dublin – but after football no two people in the same town could have less in common. You, a northside middle-class lass with a mission for truth and justice, and an inner-city boss whose life was dedicated to accumulating wealth at any cost. But as events transpired the country's top crime reporter and the most dangerous criminal would develop a mutual respect that led you to organise tickets for the Monk and his kids to a Man Utd league match which was sold out.

I remember the glee with which you told this story and the fun you got out of the fact that people in the exclusive hospitality suite that you attended after the game had no idea of the identity of the small, dark, intense-looking man with the cold eyes, who stood in the same room as some of Ireland's top property developers. You had given the Monk a pseudonym and made him repeat it so that he would not make a slip and land you totally in the shit.

If some people feel self-righteously offended by this action, they should remember that you operated in the world of trade-offs which is shared by the forces of law and order, including the police and the Special Branch, who do deals with criminal informers and paramilitaries.

Anyone who thinks that the borders between the State institutions, respectable society and the criminal underworld are clearly defined, is extremely naive. You knew that more than anyone and were actively pursuing a so-called respectable businessman, resident in Blackrock, who did regular trading in Malaysia in a less than orthodox trade.

In your usual inventive manner you managed to get a hold of a bank draft of £750,000 drawn by this individual. You tracked his movements and eventually cornered him in Dublin Airport.

He was evasive when first questioned, but got really

angry when you produced the bank draft because he knew that he was dealing with a very clever and resourceful reporter who was a real danger to him.

He protested that he was dealing in T-shirts and you replied that this sum of money would buy a hell of a lot of T-shirts. He complained about the invasion of his privacy and you replied that he should think of his part in the destruction of the privacy and lives of those hooked on drugs. In a veiled way he threatened you and ran.

Three weeks later you were meeting some colleagues for lunch in the Elephant and Castle restaurant in Temple Bar. As you glanced around the room who did you spot at a corner table but Mr T-Shirt himself. Halfway through his starter, he gulped the rest, threw money on the table and fled past a startled waitress.

Such incidents raised two questions at the end of the spectrum. Just to what extent were the so-called respectable professional classes involved in transactions helping to launder the proceeds of crime under the guise of legitimate business and how could Veronica Guerin live her life like this? You were convinced and had evidence to prove the contention that the crime bosses had the cooperation of accountants and brokers in the acquisition of property, public houses and land from money which could have come from only one source – the proceeds of criminal activity, mostly drugs and robbery. You gave me a classic example.

A well-known godfather, John Gilligan, dealer in huge quantities of stolen goods, just two years after being released from a prison sentence had accumulated enough money to purchase and develop a country mansion on big acreage worth in excess of £3 million. This man claimed to make a legitimate living from gambling, but the proceeds of betting could never explain the lavish property and lifestyle.

He built the biggest indoor equestrian centre in Europe in a field next to the house. The effect is like turning out of a little country lane to be confronted by an aircraft hangar; just a small indication of the power and wealth of this thug.

It later transpired that a financial adviser who ran a big company had been involved in laundering Gilligan's ill-gotten gains. As usual your suspicions proved to be absolutely correct.

Should a broker purchase property for an individual suspected of being a serial killer? Because that is exactly what a drugs baron is – a serial killer, feeding death to unfortunate junkies who in a very short space of time lose any choice by the strength of addiction. It was this fact that provided the central motivation for your work, as well as the added fact that most of the crime in the city was drug-related – muggings, assault and murder. But the main threat was to the children, the future generations, and you saw this as the slaughter of the innocents on whose destruction and death an empire of wealth, corruption and degeneracy was built. I understood when you asked me not to *"glamorise the bastards"* when depicting the crime godfathers.

It was appalling, in your opinion, that Ecstasy was available to twelve-year-old kids in every town and village in Ireland. This was not just moral indignation at this social outrage; the very act of getting a twelve-year-old hooked was a fact sensational enough for a journalist of

42

your integrity to mount a campaign against the fact, and the rich scum responsible for such sickening actions.

Here were the godfathers buying property, drinking in the best bars, taking two holidays a year in such exotic locations as Barbados and St. Lucia while there was a growing army of young men and women walking around our housing projects in the inner and outer city, walking around like survivors of the Holocaust, desperate for the chemical food that would keep them from death's door for just one more day.

Travelling, as we often did, down Pearse Street on the way back to town, we could see the queues of junkies getting their daily dose of methadone or physeptone. Their look was so distinctive that they could have been one large family – sunken cheeks, Malcolm Lowry pipe-thin arms and legs, matchstick men and women, concave chests. But most of all the eyes told the full extent of the horror of their existence – these eyes had seen hell and those people, if they lived to see another sunrise, would never be the same again.

I discussed the case of a teenage relative who was caught up in the rave scene and without admitting it "doing Ecstasy". He was capable of desperate mood swings, robbing and intense depression, which frequently lead to tears. To experience such sadness in the face of a teenager, body rake-thin, the eyes gouged by huge black circles is heart-rending. The kid is totally isolated, in denial and deeply miserable – all for what? A momentary high to the backdrop of a dancing crowd and the deadening bass thump of the utterly mindless music. Others died and we can't imagine the sense of loss and grief their families suffered.

"So you can understand why I am doing this job, despite the drawbacks for my life and in spite of the dangers," you said. Of course I did and despite this country's loss I still understand and I have nothing but contempt for those commentators who took the opportunity of your absence to suggest you were naive, and that it wasn't your job and all that cowardly horseshit; because by fuck they would rather face the wrath of God than make such comments in your presence. And they never had the courage to do that or to even attempt to do your job.

People have and will continue to speculate about the motivation of a woman who put herself and her family in grave danger to do her job. The speculation and the implied criticism is from a small quarter and baseless. You stated it clearly to me many times and also in print that in the absence of the legislation to deal with the drug barons by seizing their assets and crippling them with tax, it was through good investigative journalism that the way in which the barons beat the system could continue to be exposed. As you emphasised, this continued spotlighting of their activities would aggravate and seriously discommode them because they had built their empires quietly and anonymously and consequently they despise the publicity.

"It is alarming that Ecstasy is being sold to twelve-year-olds in Dublin and is available in every parish in urban and rural Ireland. I have focused my work on highlighting the lifestyles and working methods of the Drug Barons. I would love to name them but because of the legal restraints I am forced to use pseudonyms which are common among the criminal fraternity. This is not glamourising their activities but highlighting the fact that these Barons become

*millionaires. And the system does nothing to stop it. This
gall me although I am aware that the Gardaí do not have the
resources allocated to take them on in even the smallest way.
These Barons can amass huge wealth without having to
explain its source. And then they are allowed 'business' status
as 'property owners'. Part of my job is to pressurise the
government into bringing in legislation to tackle both the
Barons' business interests and properly address the lack of
facilities to deal with the addicts on the ground. There should
be asset-seizing powers and more co-operation between the
police and the Revenue Commissioners. We have highlighted
the danger of drugs and the sort of criminal that profits from
the problem and hopefully put it towards the top of the
political agenda. But at the end of the day I am a reporter and
the drug problem is part of us all."*

Your reporting also has further consequences for the
godfathers – the police are forced to address them and the
Government is being prompted to introduce legislation
to prevent unscrupulous crime bosses from amassing so
much wealth from illegal activities. To say you provided
a threat to these highly dangerous, immoral and ruthless
criminals is an understatement.

Most of them had at some time or another spent time
in prison. Having tasted the luxurious lifestyle normally
associated with captains of industry, the last thing they
wanted was to be returned to the environment of
Mountjoy Prison. Your life was in danger, all of the time
and at any time, and you knew it.

Nor were you fearless and immune to such a threat.
Shortly after you were back on the road after the
shooting, you were driving along a big open road on one
of your assignments, when your rear-view mirror

45

reflected a distant motorbike being driven by a helmeted figure. As the image got bigger in the mirror, every nerve in your body froze and it seemed that you could not get a millilitre of oxygen into your lungs, cold sweat broke out on your forehead, your body locked in paralysis.

"I began to hyperventilate, my mind froze over, I couldn't think, it was as if I was waiting for my death and there was nothing I could do but wait. Like one of those nightmares where you are being chased and there is nothing to do but be caught."

The bike rider grew to huge proportion in your mirror and then thundered by. You pulled the car onto the hard shoulder and while your whitened knuckles gripped the wheel you hyperventilated for what seemed an age.

"I stayed there . . . I didn't know whether I wanted to faint or get sick. I don't know how long it took but eventually I pulled myself together and drove on."

I was mesmerised as you recounted this incident. Again I projected myself into your place and I experienced a sense of the naked terror that gripped you for those moments. This small incident spoke volumes about the woman I knew as Veronica Guerin. Here was no super-heroine, but a human possessed of the same frailty as the rest of us.

So all the greater your courage for going on with an ever-present sense of fear which was underlined and multiplied by the brutal arrogance of the untouchables of Dublin who corrupted society like a plague and besmirched the legacy of the founding fathers of our State. Despite your fear you were determined to find out who was responsible for ordering your shooting and you eventually did, quite by accident.

We discussed the world in which you chose to operate. Criminals routinely cheat each other, trade information with each other, police and journalists. It was a web in which you became entangled. As one Special Branch man put it: "Nobody in this world has the whole picture – it is like a jigsaw – I have one part, the criminal another and Veronica perhaps two parts."

No more than at that time. There was an absolute picture, that only emerged after June 26, 1996, but one thing was sure: both you and the police had a vague idea of the real workings of the country's number one godfather – the Warehouseman (John Gilligan). In any event it is a world in which hard fact and truth are hard to grasp. There are no records – and the ones that exist are more than likely falsified. The information was largely verbal, but no less dangerous for that. The wrong word in the wrong ear could and often did lead to brutal killing. When the stakes are high, the risk and the danger increases commensurately. It was not that you were not aware of this but there was so much else to know that was even more dangerous than anyone, however close to this world, imagined. But inevitably because of your persistence you would come far too close to this kingdom of evil. In the interim there were whispered phone calls, car-park meetings, long journeys for tid-bits of information and the unrelenting search for real leads and at the end of it all, the piecing together of the information and of course the writing of the stories.

You have been accused of being obsessive, driven, and sometimes even I wondered. As the Saturday deadline approached you got less and less sleep, often abandoning it altogether on a Friday night as you put together your stories in the peaceful hours between darkness and dawn. But anyone who has worked and really understands journalism with all its pitfalls can appreciate how it can induce this passion and excitement in newspapermen and women but has its own distinct characteristics. And then when the presses rolled and your adrenalin subsided you returned again to your demi-monde of intrigue, betrayal and brutality. The one thing that your critics easily forget is that on a very basic level you were excited and fulfilled by this work – and I can still hear this phrase again and again as fresh as the first time I heard it: *"You know, I love this job, I really love it. I can't imagine doing anything else."* And that job included dealing with the Dublin criminal who was born with a double cross on his forehead: John Traynor, a motor-mouth who gave you a lot of stories and leads but who was ultimately going to betray you, as he did his former employer the General, and as he is still prepared to do in shopping his past paymaster the drug godfather (John Gilligan).

Traynor was a classic example of middle management of the new Dublin criminal breed. He grew up in a south-city housing project in Charlemont Street and started housebreaking at nine years of age. In his late twenties he got a five-year sentence for possession of firearms. He had graduated to more serious crime and did three years of a seven-year stretch in England for receiving stolen bonds. Later he ran a shop in Aungier Street which was a laundering front for the then number one godfather in the city – the General, Martin Cahill. It was while running the shop he tried to rip off Cahill who, when he found out, met Traynor in a carpark, made him get down on his hands and knees, put a gun to his temple and threatened to blow his brains out. But John Traynor was a born Judas and he did not learn a lesson from this incident. He was an informer by nature, with his only loyalty to the quick buck, and of course, he was a compulsive liar. He eventually acquired a back-street lock-up garage in Rathmines and a motor shop in Naas. His trading in cars, spare parts etc. seemed to be a basis for an ostentatious lifestyle which included an £80,000 Mercedes, a boat and third-hand racing cars. But there was more to Traynor's wealth than met the eye. His boastful braggart ways led to a loose tongue when it came to the inside track on the criminal world in Dublin. He was flattered by the attention of a female journalist and of course liked to think that he knew everything that went on in the underworld. It was another arrow to his bow, it inflated his self-image of crook-about-town, hammer-man with young girlfriend and other mistresses and frequenter of clubs and pubs. But of course his mouth and his passing of information about his criminal contemporaries would eventually spell danger for him. And one thing Traynor would prove was: that to save his own skin he would hang his own mother out to dry. While you did not trust him, there were certain things you did not believe he was capable of doing.

"He was a bit of a fuckin loud-mouth, drinker and whoremonger, but useful to me. There is no doubt that he had the contacts even if he was boastful and he liked the intrigue of talking off the record to the press. I reckoned that he must have had some information or some idea about who had me shot. I went looking for him and arranged to meet in one of his pub haunts in Harold's Cross. I decided to give him a good grilling.

He was getting very drunk and I noticed he was jittery and ill at ease, more so than was characteristic. I thought that he knew something but just wouldn't open up. He swore on everyone who was close to him that he knew nothing."

He was drinking and smoking even more heavily than usual. You stuck to coffee and your task, pushing him for some information because if anyone knew who did it, it was this man, known in the criminal fraternity as the Coach.

You sensed something – the man protested too much. His beautiful young girlfriend, of whom you were quite fond, walked into the bar, walked to the table, a serious, angry look distorting her pretty features. Her words fell like a bombshell. "How could you dare speak to this woman after what you did to her?"

Your body was seized by a sensation which resembled an electric shock. Your mind was frozen over like a lake in winter but dimly you heard his drunken reply. "Fuck you, fuck you. I'm after spending two hours trying to convince her I didn't."

Your stomach was overcome by a wave of nausea; you rushed to the toilet and got sick several times. You were physically and emotionally overcome by the enormity of the betrayal. The girlfriend comforted you and helped you clean up. When you returned to the bar, Traynor had disappeared.

It took you a while to get over this, get your head around the fact that the shooting was organised by your main criminal contact. It later emerged that he was under pressure from certain criminals who knew he was passing information to you. After all, your reporting was undermining a multi-million-pound business which had no such threat from the forces of law and order. And there was another debt to pay. The General, Martin Cahill, had let Traynor off the hook after he had tried to rip him off. But after the General was assassinated Traynor gave you the story about the godfather's sexual relationship with his wife, Frances's sister, Tina. It was in classical journalese "a great story" and an exclusive, but clearly not one which the General's family would take kindly to. The General's elder sons might take it as a slight to their mother and to the memory of their father. So Traynor was under pressure to sort that "journalist bitch" out. He took his time and waited for an opportunity which would provide a smokescreen. That presented itself with your article on the Monk which appeared in the *Sunday Independent* of January 29, 1995. If anything happened to you in the wake of that article the finger would be pointed well away from Traynor or indeed the General's family or associates. But for your determination and persistence, the truth would never have been known. Again that is a measure of your extraordinary attitude to life. Most of us would have rather not known. Eventually you took a philosophical attitude to Traynor's involvement and in a sense it gave you more control over your contact. It was a professional relationship of convenience but would turn sour when Traynor revealed his colours with an association with a much more dangerous foe – the psychopathic Warehouseman (John Gilligan). Judas is a man who never failed to live up to his name. That was partly because being a spendthrift he never did have enough money to support his degenerate lifestyle and was always open to the thirty pieces of silver.

"In a sense Traynor was a loser. He was never going to

achieve the status of the main godfathers of Irish crime. He didn't have the brains for big operations because he was always chasing his tail, he was going to be looking for crumbs off the big boys' table. In that way he was going to continue to be useful to me. He was a bit of a big eejit with an inflated idea of his own worth. A liar yes, but aren't they all?"

Sometimes I lose track of time and the present melts into the annals of the past and I feel like the chronicler of your death foretold. In a peculiar sense I was, because it was a subject that we discussed on many occasions, especially as you stepped up your campaign against the drug barons and especially the Warehouseman (John Gilligan), whose earlier criminal career was based on his ability to rob goods stored in warehouses across the city. But this was a high-risk operation and he was caught and served time in prison. He was accidentally introduced to a far more lucrative occupation by none other than your main contact, Judas himself.

John Gilligan, born in the working-class suburb of Ballyfermot in 1952, started his criminal career as a petty thief and housebreaker in the late sixties and seventies and built himself up to be the biggest, most powerful and dangerous crime and drugs baron that Ireland has ever known. His crime record over a twenty-year period, dating from October 1974 with his first six months' sentence for larceny until his release from Portlaoise prison in 1994 on a double conviction (a four-year stretch for receiving stolen goods combined with six months for assault on a chief prison officer) is littered with convictions for petty crimes. Over two decades he received a total of eight years and eight months in sentences, not all of which he served, which for a dangerous, hardened criminal is not a bad average. But on release from his last stretch in Portlaoise Prison he vowed that he would never ever spend another minute behind bars.

Within a short period of his release Gilligan was showing signs of the massive fortune he was amassing. It was known that he ran an illegal cigarette-import trade distributed by street sellers around the city and country which produced considerable profit (£2 million a year). But where did the rest of it come from? Hardly from his highly risky business of stealing large amounts of goods from warehouses. You found Gilligan to be a more than worthy subject of investigation, as such wealth could only come from one source: drugs. And this wealth was accumulated against a background fact that up to 1993 Gilligan was claiming Unemployment Benefit for his wife and two children.

Much later we discovered that it was Traynor who introduced him to the massive potential of drug-trading, from the most modest of beginnings. One time he, Traynor, was checking out one of his car imports and discovered that a substantial amount of cannabis was stored inside one of the wheels. He went to a local dealer who offered him five, meaning £500. He tried another one down the road who offered him seven – he agreed and nearly fell backwards off his bar stool when he was presented with £7000. He rang up the Warehouseman and told him that he should get into drugs as it was far more lucrative and less risky than his existing calling – robbing warehouses.

He did, and a mere two years after getting out of prison he was the lord of a country manor worth in excess of £3 million. But the Warehouseman, despite the high-society ambitions of his wife, was basically a street thug who was not able to handle the real implications of his wealth.

He became more arrogant, greedy and nasty as he tasted the fruits of his drugs trade and instead of relaxing into his new-found status and boxing clever, he became more Napoleonic, a 90's version of James Cagney in *White Heat* – he was on top of the pile and nobody was going to knock him off that perch. Realising that if he was to be caught out and returned to prison, his empire could easily fall into the hands of others, he was particularly paranoid about this possibility and thus was even more dangerous. He would stop at nothing to prevent that happening. The General was only in the handbag-snatching department when it came to the Warehouseman.

The myth that the assassination of the General in August 1994 would reduce criminal activity in Dublin was exposed as nonsense by the rise of a new and highly dangerous and ruthless criminal class whose empire and dreams of wealth were founded on drugs. One of the country's most astute detectives and arresting officer for one of his early crimes told me later that, while the Warehouseman was being questioned, he suddenly turned to the detective and coldly told him, "You will never make it to Court".

"It wasn't that I was afraid," said the officer "but the chilling realisation that I believed him. He meant what he said." He did make it to Court and the Warehouseman was put away, but he has never forgotten the impact of that vile epiphany. One day I was to experience the same awful feeling without words.

The officer went on to discuss the Warehouseman's vicious nature –

"He was always a criminal to be taken seriously because he meant what he said. While he served his time on the four-year sentence for receiving stolen goods he mixed in Portlaoise prison with the worst criminal scum this country has ever known. One [named criminal] known as the Border Fox cut off both little fingers of his ransom victim. These men were immersed in a culture of violence and took great pleasure in blood-letting. Gilligan fitted in well in this company and even tried to prove himself by a vicious assault on a head prison officer which earned him an additional six months' sentence. Even in a prison full of violent scum and paramilitaries this attack was unprecedented and proved two things about Gilligan. One, he wasn't prepared to live by any code, and two, he had no concept of the consequences of his brutal actions. But having said all that, after his release, Gilligan went to ground and out of the consciousness of the security forces. Despite his record, which overall was not that spectacular, he became an unknown quantity. Many of the police that dealt with him had retired or moved on to other areas."

Until Veronica Guerin put the finger on him.

Judas had blabbed his mouth off about the Warehouseman, so you decided to doorstep him at his country mansion despite warnings of the danger involved. People have since questioned your judgement in taking such a radical approach especially in the wake of the first shooting. I questioned them too, but you always had the right of reply. You still do, because your spirit will always be alive and in recent times I have received plenty of evidence of that fact. To keep the cynics in the unholy state of misery that is their wont, I will not reveal that evidence – let that remain between us.

The move to confront the Warehouseman can with hindsight seem to have fatal consequences, but so did everything you were doing. Remember the context – law and order was important in the face of the Untouchables and anyway hindsight is one hundred per cent vision. We talked at length about this incident and our later encounter with the Warehouseman outside a country courthouse. We have to look at the time and also the responsibility of Veronica Guerin. You were carrying a message that was inseparably linked to your personal courage. People in that rarefied category of human endeavour are not determined by the inhibitions experienced by mere mortals like me and the vast majority of the populace. Indeed we depend on such heroic figures to push back the parameters and to undertake missions on our behalf.

On Thursday September 14, 1995 when you arrived at the front door of the Warehouseman's multi-million spread you were apprehensive as the details of his vicious nature began to sink in. But never in a thousand years could you have predicted what happened next.

The door was opened and you were confronted by a small man with a tan dressed in a silk dressing-gown. You identified yourself and said you were there to ask him questions about his alleged involvement in drug- running. His face was transformed by a psychopathic rage.

The following act you described again as akin to a slow-motion sequence. He hit out at you screaming "Where's the fuckin wire?" He then ripped your blouse in an effort to find what he thought was a concealed microphone. You were back against the car at this stage and he continued to punch you and threaten your life, the life of your husband and son in the most vile and perverted fashion. You had never encountered such naked evil.

"I thought it would never end, the beating seemed to go on forever, it was horrible, frightening, much worse than the shooting."

Even in your recollection months after the event you shuddered as if the mere thought of the incident sent a shiver through your body. This brutal act summed up the attitude of this particular godfather. Without a single thought of the consequence of his action, he simply unleased a chain of violence against a woman. The thought of prison did not come into it – he was safe in the knowledge that with his wealth he could do anything without fear of recrimination. I learned later from my police contact that he had no doubt that he would have killed you there and then but was distracted by some equestrian riders nearby who could have been potential eye-witnesses. In this instance an unusual alarm-bell rang in his enraged mind. Of all the Irish crime bosses, this man was the most dangerous. He was Mr Untouchable. You were shaken to the bone by this ghastly experience and of all the violence and threats issued against you, this had the most impact.

"I was very low afterwards. The shooting contained that one moment of terror as I stared at the gun-barrel, but then everything else happened very swiftly. But the beating just went on and on and the terror never let up. It really affected me very badly".

Like the other experiences you recounted, I again put myself in your place and I was frozen by fear and the thought of where it had happened – in the middle of nowhere with no recourse to any kind of value support – even a passing motorist. I felt the shock and the delayed trauma and the utter loathing and the humiliation that haunts the victim of violence.

I look now at the photograph that was taken of you as part of the evidence of a potential assault case and I can see all those feelings in your unutterably sad expression. Gone is the radiant smile. There is a bruise under the left eye – your eyes lack the sparkle that did miraculously return as you recovered from the beating.

Overall there is an expression of puzzlement as if you are saying to yourself – "What the fuck is this all about and is anything worth this?" Those thoughts did cross your mind constantly in the aftermath. But while the immediate effects wore off in time, I believe that you never really mentally recovered from the horror of the beating meted out by the Warehouseman, and the memory prompted you to take an assault case against him in the face of apathy in the police, which forced you to go right to the top to have this monster pursued through the court.

"I had to go right to the top to get anything done . . . When eventually there was some movement on the case it still took two of my Special Branch mates to make an arrangement to meet Gilligan and inform him that an assault case was being taken against him. I had never come across a criminal who inspired so much fear, particularly among the community on which he had imposed himself. This man thought he was untouchable and if everyone else was going to go along with

it, I wasn't. Nobody deserves to get away with beating a woman."

It is yet another measure of your courage that you could continue your work with such determination. Not simply courage but bravery in the face of the most vile and pernicious evil. I told you again and again that I could not understand how you could do a job which intrinsically is difficult, demanding and stressful without the added burden of danger.

Your reply was simple: *"I love this job and someone has to take these barons on or our society will be totally corrupted."*

"It wasn't just me, I was representing all the other victims of violence in the land."

It is another beautiful summer's day. On the pond the reflection of the sun is sparkling on the water and the tiny slivers of light are jumping up from the liquid surface. I think of you as part of every aspect of that visual beauty and try to get away from the reality of your cold grave. I have seen pictures of the headstone in the papers but I have never stood before it. Perhaps this is a form of denial. If so it is an unreality with which I feel comfortable. I know that the only thing that is left is your spirit and that is as real as the waters of the pond and I recognise that the aspects of your colourful spirit are as golden as anything that nature can express.

As the cool days of fading spring blew the exquisite cherry blossoms from the trees like floating snowdrops and gradually gave way to the steel-blue skies of the summer, we met less frequently but with no less intensity.

One encounter I will never forget – in Buswell's Hotel, late afternoon. It was a meeting I looked forward to with a familiar sense of anticipation, the feeling of being in the company of one of the most charismatic, witty and intelligent human beings I have had the privilege to meet.

We have all harboured fantasies, usually inspired by fictional characters, of stepping into the shoes of a hero, the main man or woman. Of course, the fantasies come without the reality of living in the solitary and spirit-breaking role of the maverick. We have all wanted to be a Serpico, a Woodward or a Bernstein without the price that has to be paid in risk or the consequences of something going horribly wrong.

There lies the difference between illusion and reality, between Veronica Guerin and the rest of us. You were a true heroine.

My meeting with you happened to overlap with an appointment with Feargal Quinn on whom you were writing an article in the Trading Places mode.

With your innate ability to move ahead of the journalistic posse, you revealed that a Fianna Fáil survey, conducted in preparation for the next election, showed that 87% of those interviewed identified crime as the main priority for political action.

You then outlined to Feargal Quinn, who is a Senator as well as a highly successful businessman, the hold that the crime bosses and drug barons had over the city and country. It is no exaggeration to say that he was utterly shocked by the import of your knowledge and the apparent impotence of Government and Gardaí to deal with a situation in which murder had become commonplace. You had always said that you were appalled that murder had become such a familiar part of life and even the media was starting to downgrade its news value. Our conversation ranged over many topics including your *modus operandi*.

Many times you told me, without a hint of pomposity, that you had never and would never write anything that was ever a scintilla off the truth.

"People want to write things that are part of an agenda, usually their agenda – and that applies to all sides of the equation, police and criminals. Well, there are times you get it wrong – not deliberately – you just get led up the garden path. But you have to be wise and vigilant. If you play ball ultimately nobody will respect you, not even the people with the agendas. I always try to differentiate and tell the truth."

No one can quibble about your bravery. Fear is the constant companion of the brave. I will, until my dying day, admire how you put behind you the natural instinct of flight and stayed on to fight.

There are journalists and commentators who will interpret this as naiveté. If one is realistic about danger – one should simply take flight. But as you have often pointed out – police are in constant danger on a daily basis as part of their job and yet if one backed off as a result of intimidation or pressure he or she would be perceived by society as a coward. In Sicily the great anti mafia prosecutors, Giovanne Falcone and Paulo Bonsellino, lived for many years knowing their fate was assassination but they continued fighting for a better society until their deaths. Were they mad? Fool hardy? No, they were brave men. As Veronica Guerin stood up to such intimidation some people retrospectively perceive her as a fool. Their view has no logic or sense and is not shared by the ordinary people of Ireland. You outlined what you and indeed our whole society was up against.

"Dublin has become a war zone, a battleground for ruthless criminals and drug-dealers. Inner-city areas are ravaged by the effects of heroin. AIDS and violence and death abound. How can a crime reporter stand back from this? You might as well ask a war correspondent to stop reporting the war."

The Warehouseman (John Gilligan), had threatened to kill you and your neighbours and sexually assault your son Cathal. This threat had been used both during the assault and in a telephone call to you afterwards. Later again he offered you £1 million to drop the case. We did not know at the time the real extent of this man's burgeoning empire and the ruthless private army he had built to prop up and protect it. But his actions provided sufficient reason for caution and I wondered whether by pushing this assault charge, you were in fact pushing your luck.

We travelled to Kilcock, a small rural town an hour's drive from Dublin, for the court hearing on the assault. I had breakfast with you and Graham in the house beforehand. On the way, one of the car tires punctured and we joked that the Warehouseman had probably been responsible for tampering with it in an effort to put you out of action for the court hearing. We chatted and talked about various things on the way. I did not detect in you, but I myself certainly felt, the odd wave of apprehension.

Being a film correspondent, I live a lot of my life at the back of a theatre watching illusory representations of life being played out on the silver screen. I encounter a lot of celluloid violence set in underworld arenas such as

Scorcese's *Goodfellas* and *Casino* with Joe Pesci's performances as psychopathic criminal Mafia types – you know, hammering the shit out of some shivering small fry – fuck you, fuck you – *Bam*.

I'm not saying that Scorcese does not treat the subject seriously – he does, but despite the violent traits of the characters that Pesci portrays, you can get a bit of a laugh out of him. As you can with Travis Bickle in *Taxi Driver* – the guy is fuckin bonkers, a violent psycho, but who can resist repeating the scene when he looks in the mirror and says – "You talkin to me?" Or when he shoves his gun into the stomach of Jodie Foster's pimp, played by Harvey Keitel, pulls the trigger and says "Suck on this". But, however convincing, what you see is a movie – however brilliantly staged. But like Michael Herr wrote about Vietnam, you have to keep reminding yourself – that this ain't the movies.

The blood on the streets of Dublin is real. Well, on this day, a beautiful warm day with a lovely sky, I was going to get an object lesson between reality and illusion in the criminal underworld. We arrived in the small town, almost more accurately a village, and crossed the bridge to the "court" which is a local health centre doubling up as the centre of administration of justice, as in many rural Irish towns. There we were met by a photographer from the *Sunday Independent* and a member of the Special Branch who had acted as one of the arresting officers. The place was such a nondescript venue for a case with such deep significance for the future security of the Irish nation and the battle against the new breed of crime barons.

Two dark-coloured Pajero jeeps pulled up on the

opposite side of the road outside the courthouse. The Warehouseman (John Gilligan), alighted from one with a number of lieutenants, his wife and daughter from another. I looked at you. You began to tremble as if an ice-cold wind had blown across the forecourt. "Are you alright?" I asked.

"I'm just shaking at the thought of having to face that bastard across the courtroom and go through it all again." The skin on your face was tightly drawn over your cheekbones and your eyes had that faraway look of a person sinking deeply into the dark pool of remembrance. What you faced was a vivid recreation of what was then the worst nightmare of your life as the victim of a brutal attack. God knows in this country, born and weaned in its earliest years on violence and bloodshed, we have had more than our share of victims. The reports in the newspapers and other media, however comprehensive, only give an inkling of the suffering involved. And now you, the standard-bearer, would have to relive the trauma of those frightening moments and the helpless state of humiliation which follows. My heart went out to you because I could sense every pulse of your vulnerability.

I went into the body of the courtroom and got the photographer to come out. As the Warehouseman crossed the forecourt the photographer fired off about six shots from hip level. The criminal godfather was smaller than I imagined but danger emanated from his squat frame. He stood up on the steps of the court and eye-balled us through the slit eyes in his fleshy face. Two of his lieutenants, one with a big belly, the other dark, sallow and mean-lean, eyed us from the other side, their mobile phones held like guns in a subtle threatening fashion. You shivered again as you caught the Warehouseman's gaze. He then turned away and consulted with his solicitor, a member of a well-known Dublin legal family. I held nothing against him, he was doing his job but I wondered if he could also detect the pernicious evil emanating from his client; so tangible that the photographer made a request to be allowed to leave now that we had the godfather on celluloid. Sensing his fear, you relaxed and promised to ring him on his mobile when he was halfway to Dublin. I understood his fear because I was gripped by it – not even the presence of an armed policeman gave me the slightest consolation. I felt I was in the presence of a man who literally owned the territory and would deal out unmerciful punishment for trespassing, as he had already done to you.

Now I understood how cowardly I was – I had never received any direct threat or been beaten and here I was with my knees knocking because I was obsessed by the thought that he wouldn't think twice about wiping us all out on the way back from the hearing. I disguised all this from you because I did not want to be seen to be letting Veronica Guerin down, especially when I saw the fear also etched in your eyes and body language. But inside, believe me, I was rattling. When the hearing was ultimately adjourned, the only reason I was not paralysed by panic was that the armed policeman offered to drive ahead of us on a quicker back-road route to Dublin. We stopped for lunch at a pub in Castleknock and I had a long and interesting conversation with the Special Branch man about his activities and your place in the losing battle against crime. He was full of admiration for your skill and courage and confirmed what you had told me about having to go to the top to get the assault charge pursued. He also confirmed that the Warehouseman had built up a hugely lucrative business – from the sale of stolen and illegally imported cigarettes alone he was taking in two million a year.

"There is," he told me, "a certain amount we know about this man, but there is also a lot we don't know and probably never will because the politicians and top police brass are blind to the present desperate situation and people like me who would love to do something are impotent and disillusioned. Veronica is really doing a great job exposing these godfathers but she should not be doing it alone."

This man had been part of your protection squad after the first shooting, before being dismissed by you. I questioned him about the logic or lack of it in your approach in getting rid of your protectors.

"Well, I don't have to agree with it or disagree," he said, "but from Veronica's viewpoint I can see the sense. It has to do with the way she operates and it is certainly true that no criminal would deal directly with her if armed detectives are only yards away. In fact it might be more dangerous if they thought that Veronica was being used to set them up. I am not saying that this would ever happen but it could be the criminal perception."

Later you drove me back to the *Sunday Independent*. The dark shroud had been removed from your shoulders, you chatted merrily, the sparkle was back in your eye. Extraordinarily you had put the fear and loathing behind you. It still clung to me. Perhaps your veteran status helped you recover more quickly as well as the fact that there was always another crime story to pursue but the earlier incident underlined your vulnerability and the fact that you were not superhuman but experienced fear like every other human being.

Your great gift was that you had the ability to conquer it. In the primeval stakes I was the opposite. It was flight not fight that showed me I was born to run. For days afterwards the cynicism, arrogance and utter contempt for decency displayed by this criminal haunted me and I knew that soon I would have to reveal my deep-seated fear of this man and what he could potentially do to you.

Another time during a visit to a prisoner in Mountjoy, your name came up in conversation. The prisoner told me he shared a meal table with the first lieutenant of a dead crime boss (the General). This man had a reputation for toughness and extreme violence while a leader of an armed-robbery gang. As he was approaching the end of a long sentence he had clearly re-established contact with leading members of the criminal fraternity with the view to making some money after his release.

One day at the meal-table he made reference to your role as a crime reporter in exposing the godfathers. "If she is acting as judge and jury to unconvicted people, can she complain if they act as judge and jury to her?"

I clearly went pale at the implied threat in this statement. The prisoner leaned across the table. "I'm only telling you how this guy is thinking which means a consensus has been reached by the underworld bosses in regard to Veronica's reporting. I think you should pass this message on to her and I hope she takes heed."

I thanked him and later made by way back to the *Sunday Independent*. The phrase weighed heavily upon me. There was a coolness about it which put the hairs up at the back of my neck. Being a born coward, I took it seriously.

Far from being a crude threat it contained what I perceived as chilling logic, a simple justification for stopping the work of a reporter. It was a political statement from the underworld with reverberations of paramilitary utterances on violent intent. The fact that these people can justify any course of action to themselves is what makes them dangerous. I was, to put it mildly, worried about your safety.

I recounted the statement to *Sunday Independent* news editor Willie Kealy. He took it seriously and asked me to be sure to pass it on directly to Veronica.

I rang you and you just laughed.

"Don't worry, Mick, because I am not worrying." You had this disarming charm which would defuse a seemingly serious situation and I just relaxed and well, put it out of my mind.

The reality of such threats is light years in difference from the portrayal of the mob in *Goodfellas*, but I have little doubt that the swaggering barons try to model themselves on their celluloid counterparts.

A video copy of *The Bronx Tale* was found in the General's car after he had been assassinated. But I advise the present crop of criminals to consult the video shop again and they will find that the mob don't swagger, they prefer to work underground so as not to attract public wrath.

They understand that once they write their names in blood, they sign their own death warrant.

We discussed this aspect of criminality and life – in simple terms what goes around comes around – the ever-revolving circle of life and death, the crime which never escapes the punishing law of nature.

But the Dublin godfathers were becoming so rich and

powerful that they were blinded and rendered immune to the inevitable consequences of their actions. That is with the exception of the Monk who received intimations of mortality when his close friend and mentor Paddy Shanahan was shot.

The General was mercilessly gunned down according to the prevailing wisdom because he had the arrogance to tell the Provisional IRA to fuck off when they tried to arrange a meeting to discuss possible links with the loyalists who planted a bomb unsuccessfully at The Widow Scallan's.

The General made another mistake – he tried to set up the Monk in the same operation which suggested strongly that he had communicated with the loyalists. You were convinced that this action provided the key to the General's fate. It was a constant source of amazement that most of the main criminal players were not taking into account that their actions could have consequences for themselves.

"On the one hand they are intoxicated with their own power. They drive big cars and hard bargains, hang out in clubs with their younger lieutenants who are also making money beyond their dreams. The more money they make, the less they think they have to fear. And if they order a hit they do it in the absolute certainty that they won't have to pay the normal price society demands – life in prison. After twelve or more gangland assassinations, no convictions. They are literally getting away with murder. And the more that goes on, the less value life has. The small-time drug-dealer Gerry Lee, who is a bit of a nasty piece of work, is celebrating his birthday at a party with family and friends in Coolock. The drinking goes on to 7am and suddenly a gunman walks in the open back door, walks up to

Lee and shoots him twice in the head. That's how easy it is and that is how casual the killers and their masters have become. At the same time as this is going on the Minister for Justice, Nora Owen, is rejecting the suggestion that the number of murders is growing. These are not like most murders of a violent domestic nature, these are contract killings carried out on behalf of or by a new powerful criminal class who simply don't have to worry about the consequences of their actions. This rash of crime will eventually come to the top of the political agenda of the ordinary voter but until then the politicians continue to ignore the dangers."

Some weeks after our encounter with the Warehouseman outside the court, I was overcome with a sense of foreboding. I felt you were in danger more than any time in your short career. I remembered the conversation I had had with the member of the Special Branch who had protected you in the wake of the first shooting and had arrested the Warehouseman for the assault. We had spoken about the apathy at the top level in the force and total neglect of the situation by politicians who, despite the huge escalation in drug-running and killing, seemed to be totally unaware of the threat to society.

You and I met and discussed those issues and in particular the threat posed to you by the assault case against a criminal who had vast wealth and power and whose record proved that he had no grasp of the consequences of his actions. Already he had not only threatened you in the most vile fashion, but also offered you a million pounds to drop the case. A man who makes a serious offer like this is determined not to go back to prison and thus is capable of anything.

When you told me about the monetary offer, I must have overreacted. "Jesus Christ," I uttered, "that's fuckin serious."

That mischievous expression took over your face. *"Yeah, I'll take it and fuck all this hassle. Myself and Graham and Cathal will all go off to live in the Bahamas."*

"A man that makes that offer is both serious and mad," I proferred. "You have to take it seriously."

"Ah, go and shite," you said and in metaphorical terms I did.

Veronica, you had that sort of effect on people who were concerned. I'm all hyped up with a sense of fear and foreboding one minute, the next I'm laughing away. The moment passed but I had to come back to it later.

Judas (Traynor) had told you that Gilligan was contrite and sorry for his action but you were determined to press the case through to its conclusion. I argued that the danger to you far outweighed any outcome of the case, which after all could go any way. You replied that if you dropped the case, where would that put the ordinary citizen in the role of victim of violence? You said that your role was to lead by example and not show that you backed off in the face of intimidation. But I had seen the bloated face of evil and I was afraid for myself but mostly for you.

"They'll shoot you in the head this time," I said, with a feigned calmness which disguised my desperation.

"Don't worry," you replied, *"I'll be alright."*

"How, who will look after you?"

"Someone will," you said reassuringly.

"Who?"

"The Monk will look after me."

I argued that these people look after nobody but themselves. We talked on for an hour or two about the script which I had been developing over the period of our discussions. We agreed that the main character would be a woman journalist, investigating the Dublin crime world and already we had copperfastened the other main players.

You saw the project as an extension of your work which of course contained a considerable element of drama – fact being often stranger than anything that could be dredged up by fiction.

In the face of real events and dangers, the script paled into insignificance, but then, as now, I knew that fate had a hand in this collaboration and in some sense I would be both a chronicler and guardian of something and somebody very special.

As the cloudy unpredictability of May merged into the orange sunlight and deep blue skies of June, I began to flesh out the story of a woman journalist taking on the crime bosses of the Dublin underworld and attempting to save a society which was under a bigger threat than any posed over the years by the paramilitaries.

The months of work began to bear fruit. You told me that you were going to *"out"* Judas for being involved in drugs. I urged caution – there was no need to name him and because of his mouth it could be more dangerous than it would seem on the surface. If any cornered rat would bite, it would be him.

He had close connections (closer than we knew at the time) to the Warehouseman, a man who would not hesitate to kill to keep himself out of prison and protect his empire, the worth of which we could only guess, but that judging by his lifestyle was huge.

There was another member of the unholy triumvirate – Dutchy Holland, whose presence we did not know about but who had a reputation as a cold-blooded killer who had a very good reason to do the Warehouseman's bidding.

Judas warned you not to tangle with the Warehouseman – he was capable of doing anything. His record proved it. While in prison he attacked the Head Warden, an action never contemplated by the most dangerous inmates and members of the IRA and INLA. Of course, the wardens exacted appropriate punishment but it indicated that here was a man who acted first and thought afterwards.

But you were on a mission and like Socrates nothing would deter you, not even the mortal danger which was your ever-present partner. This danger was amplified by the fact related to us by diligent and committed members of the police force that there was no will at the top to deal with drug barons and the crime godfathers.

But the politicians were equally to blame. The Drug Squad was totally underfunded and the Murder Squad, which had been disbanded after the Kerry Babies case, should have been reformed in response to the alarming increase in both domestic murder and gangland killings. The crime scenes and body-bags and bodies which we were used to experiencing in books, on TV crime dramas or stories from far-flung cities of the U.S. were now a regular feature of our news bulletins and newspapers and were setting a new precedent in Irish journalism.

Strangely this practice caused little adverse comment, as if the media and the public were in the same grip of apathy as the police top brass and the politicians. Thus Veronica Guerin was very much alone in the pursuit of her mission and all the more vulnerable for that.

I went on holidays with Ger the end of the first week of June, 1996. Earlier we had discussed our plans – you hoped to get a good holiday later in the summer in the Bahamas minus the £1 million! – I would get mine out of the way and we would continue our deliberations on the script. Already we had a great deal of material and I had ninety scenes on paper.

I returned from Crete on the Sunday of June 23. I rang you on Monday to arrange to go to another hearing of the assault case against the Warehouseman on the list for the following morning. You told me that it had been postponed to another date. I promised to round up a posse of media for that hearing. The Warehouseman should know that there was more than one journalist interested in his activities. Amazingly you asked me if the rest of the media would be really interested. "That bastard beat the shit out of you," I said. "Of course they would be interested – we should have gathered an army for the first hearing."

You were more worried about our appearance at Naas Court on the Wednesday – for speeding. *"If I lose my licence,"* you said, *"I'm fucked, I won't be able to continue my work."*

"You'll be fine," I said. "The police may not like what you are doing but they will not put you off the road."

I suggested we meet after the court case at our usual place, Café Java in Leeson Street. You had an appointment with the newspaper's lawyers, so that was out. Wednesday evening then?

"What sort of fuckin eejit are you?" you said giggling. *"What's happening on Wednesday evening?"*

The penny dropped – "The semi-finals of the

European Championship – England and West Germany."

"If you think I am going to miss that match to talk about crime, you can go and shite."

We laughed and you were in great form. We would meet on Thursday at the usual place. I was to ring you at home on Tuesday night just to confirm.

Tuesday morning revealed a classically beautiful summer's day. I sat out on the balcony and worked on the script. Young courting couples lay out in the park adding a brown shade to their fresh skin.

The chestnut tree, which is as bare as a whippet in winter was in full bloom, a high-rise home for a host of chirping, fluttering, nesting birds. The shimmering waters of the pond were punctuated by the fish jumping for flies and a pair of ducks, followed by a flotilla of downy chicks. The ocean-blue sky was scarred by the thin white line of a jet trail.

You know how a smell or a sound or a sight can bring you back to another time, the summer of your youth. Long heady days of unending activity and perpetual motion, sharp sights and tastes and an appetite, what an appetite for life!

What the hell happens to us in the meantime? Is the world changing or is it us getting older, more aware of the cesspits that underpin the apparent respectable institutions of the State? What evil causes greed, avarice, ruthlessness and violence, to replace the state of grace of childhood?

Shakespeare comes to mind –

> *"If there be nothing new, but that which is*
> *Hath been before, how are our brains beguiled,*
> *Which, labouring for invention, bear amiss*
> *The second burden of a former child!"*

That is, I think, what you are trying to do, replace the evil face of Ireland with a state of grace.

I wonder why you are so alone in this pursuit, so isolated in this mission. The aroma of summer dissipates those thoughts and danger seems to reside in another country. On Tuesday night, June 25, I cannot get through on your land-line, it is constantly engaged. Eventually that night I get through on your mobile. The sound begins to break up.

"Mick," you say, *"Mick,"* and then your voice shatters into sound pieces and fades away – I can hear you dimly calling. For no reason I get a sense of foreboding. (I am a superstitious person and am prone to consider certain events as a sign. Now with hindsight I take this as an omen). Nothing to support this but a feeling. Still there is Thursday and I get back to work on the script – I want lots to talk about during our next meeting.

At about five minutes past one on Wednesday afternoon the phone rang. The hushed voice of a colleague imparted the news.

"Veronica has been shot dead on the Naas dual carriageway."

I feel the colour drain from my face, a wave of nausea washes through my stomach.

"Thanks," I say in a haze of shock. My shaking hand replaces the receiver. I am shocked, I am devastated, but I am not surprised.

The bastards might as well have shot Ireland. The nation's heart bleeds. The unthinkable has happened. My brain boils, I felt at one remove from reality. The news bulletins come and go. I am in the office and pass by shocked, pale faces. *The Sunday Independent* offices, normally a hum of activity, are like a morgue, the journalists float by like ghosts, through the windows shafts of June sunlight pour in. One of the greatest heat waves in our history suddenly takes on a mocking aspect, becomes meaningless. The heavens should weep, our blood should freeze, nature should be paralysed, but the sun shines and the sky is a reflection of an azure-ocean deep, deep blue.

Everywhere there are distant voices but nothing seems to properly connect. My heart is torn between grief and anger. Through the haze I see your chariot, the car I had travelled in with you on many an occasion, covered by a plastic sheet and surrounded by police tape. No, surely not, this is a nightmare, they couldn't, they shouldn't, they didn't shoot the messenger.

My mind is fractured with disconnected thoughts torn by conflicting emotions. Grief and revenge shadow-box in a ring of disbelief.

Our meditations on the subject of unnatural death never really included the utter reality of this eventuality. How can this be? But you predicted it and I saw it – the arrogance of the criminal fraternity proved to be boundless.

I thought of *Hamlet*, a version of which I had directed at the Project Theatre in 1993. I thought the cast and I had a unique insight into the universal genius of Shakespeare but now I recognised just how shallow our vision was, how little we really knew about the real meaning of the words. Now I understood the emotions of the ghost railing and weeping and crying for revenge for his most foul and unnatural murder. Here was a tale unfolding that would –

"Make thy two eyes, like stars, start from
 their spheres,
 Thy knotted and combined locks to part,
 And each particular hair to stand an end,
 Like quills upon the fretful porpentine."

77

Oh, did I now understand the meaning and empathise with Hamlet's lust for revenge –

"Hast me to know't, that I, with wings as swift
As meditation or the thoughts of love,
May sweep to my revenge."

There was such an undercurrent at an editorial meeting at which your colleagues were allotted individual articles in your memory.

There was some shit talked. One good writer suggested that journalists should not be doing the work of the police. I had to reply. I know you would have laughed and said to go and shite – but I pointed out that one of the reasons Veronica was doing her work was because the police lacked the will, the resources and Government backing. But overall the feeling was one of unanimity and the desire to both honour you and help complete your mission.

As always there was an element of farce. One of our famous commentators was proposing to head a journalistic task force to take on the crime barons. I giggled at his naiveté. Ah well, I know you had a good laugh listening to this nonsense, apart from the fact that the self-appointed battalion commander failed to turn up on our first mission. I had to say it – "There is only one Veronica Guerin – forget it."

I wandered through the streets of the town you loved so well, the capital of the country you died for, like the ghost of Hamlet's father. I saw people but they didn't see me or feel my loss and grief. Who could blame them? But I was isolated and it was unfair because later I would realise that, like the death of JFK, the whole nation would remember precisely what they were doing when they received the news of your death. I found myself in a pub with my partner Ger and solicitor Ronan Sheehan who had been with our project from the beginning.

The European semi-final between England and West Germany which you had looked forward to – it might as well have been a Sunday park game because I could dredge up not the slightest interest. Tears poured down Ger's cheeks like the waterfall in Powerscourt. She had never met you but, like the rest of the nation, she knew you.

Over and over the image of your car haunted me, and my imagination worked overtime. I hoped against hope that the gunman spared you any moment of terror by coming like a bolt from the blue. You had been chatting happily to a number of people before the awful event, on a high because you had escaped the driving offence with a £100 fine. It was high summer, you were happy.

Later I had this vision: you stop along the road beside a bright yellow cornfield so well-hewed by nature that it could have been a painting by a master. Above the field a canopy of ocean-blue sky. As you gaze at the field, in the distance a little girl comes into focus. She has long golden locks flowing to her shoulders and wears a snow-white dress. She runs freely on a path through the corn and you run with her down memory lane, the corn brushes against your legs and the warm breeze kisses your flushed cheeks. As the girl comes closer you recognise her steel-blue eyes and the cut of her determined chin. She then flops down on the earth and above the corn you watch with her the infinity of the sky. Birds rise from a tree, a rabbit stands stock still, stiffened by instinct, an otter slides seamlessly into the watery reeds of a river. You close your eyes and breathe in the rich aroma of summer. And then you look again and she is gone. You drive on still in the grip of a golden memory.

Then the ugly evil bastard struck, determined to strike terror in your heart, before he gunned one of the greatest women this country has ever produced down like a dog.

I didn't know then what I know now, but as I did during the months of our collaboration, I put myself in your place and I died a thousand times.

The game played on the television but it might as well have been white noise. Tears still continued to flow down Ger's cheeks and she pleaded with me to abandon the script. I couldn't, I replied. In life and in death I had a moral obligation to Veronica, I could not turn my back on this work, which she regarded as an exciting extension of her own mission, just because of some perceived danger from the people I had faced across the forecourt of a rural court. I knew then who was responsible – Lord of the Flies – the Warehouseman.

I could understand Ger's anxiety and it was her challenge that defined exactly what I had to do – continue our work as a monument and dedication to a woman who had paid with her life for her beliefs. All our hearts were like seeping open bleeding wounds, our minds a blur like a foggy November day.

The nation wept, flowers by the lorry-load from the ordinary people of the country found their way to the offices of the *Sunday Independent* and in protest to the apathy of politicians outside the gates of The Government Seat, The Dáil. Offices and factories all over the country halted for a minute's silence in respect to your memory. If there was any consolation in those dark days it was the scream of agony that came from the Irish nation and I personally vowed that your message would never be forgotten and would be spread to the world.

I wrote about the fear and loathing of our encounter with the Warehouseman whom I was convinced would kill you. He threatened to kill another reporter so I was asked if I wanted my by-line put on the article – I had no choice, as I did not have with the film project – yes. And again the following week.

In the interim the funeral ceremony – your son Cathal at the top of the church with Graham. Graham gave a wonderful speech of shining, heartrending simplicity. I tried to avoid the coffin and the finality. The church was bursting at the seams. The tears would have burst the banks of the Liffey.

The politicians whose apathy created the vacuum that you filled so magnificently sat in the pews, their heads bowed. I could see the guilt in their eyes. If they had acted even marginally on the situation you had uncovered, perhaps we would not have been sitting in the church mourning our Guardian Angel. It took your death to prompt them to take on the criminal godfathers in general and the gang that killed you in particular. I looked at the unmasked politicians and I whispered: "Fuck you, too little, too late."

Outside I hugged Graham and he said, "Don't let the bastards get away with it." The words I had committed to paper were my weapons. The Warehouseman was trying to prove that the sword was mightier than the pen. He was going to be proved wrong. Paul Williams, crime reporter of *The Sunday World*, was there wearing dark glasses and a well-cut blue suit.

Paul looked cool but he was shattered and wondered if he would be next. In the coming months not only did he prove that he was prepared to take up where you left off but he relentlessly pursued the men who planned and executed your killing. I know you are proud of him. Many times afterwards he was placed under 24-hour police protection, he was a frightened man.

As I was, in the wake of your death. I didn't know how much they knew about us and I knew for sure that they had scared the shit out of me outside the court. It might please them to know this but I am not ashamed because they are just as cowardly as I am, and as I write, they know exactly what the true nature of fear means.

On the Sunday after your death, your own newspaper would have also made you proud. It was a historic edition, never to be surpassed, and broke all the rules, leaving the public in no doubt who was responsible for Veronica Guerin's killing.

In that edition I wrote that if the criminal godfathers wanted to emulate the Mafia they should remember that once they sign their name in blood they sign their own death warrant. And so it turned out with the Warehouseman and his gang, now scattered like autumn leaves – he, himself and the man that pulled the trigger are now in custody. Judas is in Spain and fast running out of money. Tosser, who drove the bike, is in England with his sidekick "Fatso" Peter Mitchell. But none of them will get a good night's sleep because they have been sentenced to death by the Provisional IRA. The commanding officer who issued the sentence has stated that no matter where the gang reside – abroad or England or here – they will be dealt with. Even prison will not provide a safe haven – his phrase is chilling: *"They are dead men."*

I am looking at a photograph of the man who pulled the trigger – no, I'll rephrase that – the pathetic coward who made sure that you were terrified before unleashing the bullets. He has been responsible for other deaths and he was the one missing part of the Warehouseman's jigsaw, which nobody found until it was too late.

Nobody, including the police, knew that this man was a partner in the Warehouseman's operation and was shipping 180 kilos of cannabis a week and was in possession of wealth way beyond his dreams. He was part of a £100 million business, a long way from his origins as a lone bank robber – a master of disguise, who was once uncharacteristically caught counting his money at a table in the Burlington Hotel. His "company" was in the recent past able to put in a £1.3 million bid for a County Wicklow property.

He is, by standards of criminals, an old man whose bald head is pockmarked by the remaining tracks of failed hair transplants. Irony upon irony, he is a Holy Mary – doesn't drink, doesn't smoke and is a regular attender at Sunday Mass; all of which absolutely provides no inhibition when it comes to depriving a human of life.

One might imagine that the religion would have impressed some small measure of mercy in his mind. But no, he relished inspiring terror in his victim's heart. This man is merciless.

He smashed the window of your car with a metal implement to give you the moment of terror, an instant of pleading, before delivering his message – "Fuck you, bitch" before pulling the trigger.

The days after your passing merge into a labyrinth of

thoughts, feelings and emotion. I bump into the corners of the kitchen and drop cups. I walk through the serpentine passage of time like a blind man. I experience everything and see nothing.

I can't remember what day it was, such was the fog on my mind. But the impact on your family was graphically and heartrendingly expressed by Graham on a lunchtime news interview by RTE news presenter Sean O'Rourke.

Graham had gone to identify the body of his beloved wife and Cathal was staying with his grandmother. His father returned with the parish priest, Declan Doyle to impact the news to his son. Everytime I picture this scenario a vice grips my heart and Graham's account must have opened floodgates of tears. Like his speech in the church he delivered it with an utter simplicity and dignity which served to underline the tragic nature of the scene. But at the same time gave us comfort.

"I sat down on the chair and said, 'How are things?' And he said, 'Grand, Dad.'

He had been kept away from the television and the papers and nobody had said anything to him. So I said, 'Cathal, do you remember the last time Mum was shot? Well, it's happened again.'

And he said. 'Yeah? Where was she shot this time?'

And I said, 'She was shot in the heart.' And he came over and sat on my knee and he comforted me.

Declan said to him, 'Cathal, can you make a courthouse?' And Cathal said, 'Yeah.' And we made the courthouse in Naas and we made two cars and a motorbike, and then he asked, 'Who was on the motorbike?'

And I said, 'Well, there were two men on the motorbike,

and they seem to have been wearing black helmets, and they pulled up alongside Mum, and they shot into the car and hit Mum.'

'Where did they hit Mum?'

And I said, 'They hit Mum three times around the heart, and they hit her in the neck.'

'Is Mum coming home?'

And I said, 'No she's not coming home, but she's going to be here minding us, because remember, we talked about this before?'

'Oh, I got it,' he said. 'She's with God now and she'll be looking down on me and everything I do from now on.'

And it's been like that ever since, that everything we discuss, Mum has always been there and always will be. And we left there, my mother's house, and we went to Stafford's funeral home, and Veronica was there, and we had a chat and a cuddle and a laugh, like we always did, the three of us together. And we talked, and Cathal was saying, 'Mum, you're very cold' and things like this. And then we left."

I contrast the tragic beauty of this account and the intrinsic goodness of human nature expressed by Graham, Declan Doyle and the utter innocent Cathal with the foul evil souls of the men that would put a man and a boy in a situation deprived of wife and mother forever. I just cannot get my head around this and I discuss my outrage with our mutual friend Detective Gerry O'Carroll who ironically was first on the scene. "Nothing surprises me about such heartless bastards," he says. "I once arrested a man who, during a robbery, just a short time before had shot down a married security man like a dog. The act was totally unnecessary but he did it without a hint of remorse. I was questioning him in the station and asked him how his children would feel if they were without their father for Christmas. He looked at me with contempt across the table and said, 'My children are scum'. I was shocked and appalled that there was such a low example of depravity, a man that would insult his children in this way. This is just one example of the scum we are dealing with on a daily basis."

Some weeks later we return to Kilcock courthouse for the striking out of the assault case against the Warehouseman (John Gilligan). I remember talking to you the Monday before the awful event and when I said we would get all the press radio and television reporters to the next hearing of the case, you wondered would they be interested. Today, irony of all ironies, they are all here.

The health centre in Kilcock bears as much resemblance to a court as Green Street to the Taj Mahal. It is a small, shabby, one-storey building on the right-hand side as you come over the bridge in the town. There is a generous tarmacadam forecourt but once inside there is an air of cheapness. The walls are a sickly colour and the furniture looks as if it has been rescued from a skip.

This is the district court where daily dramas are enacted which might seem trivial to hardened journalists or criminals but are of major significance to the participants. The majority of cases concern traffic offences.

From an improvised bench the judge delivers his decisions in a mantra – fine, endorse, fine, 20 days for default, disqualification. There are two young men handcuffed to tall, good-looking guards dressed in casual but fashionable manner. It is as clear as the little daylight that enters this space that the defendants are already serving a sentence and, by their looks, come from the wrong side of town. The air of depression in this primitive chamber, whose dun walls are covered with a series of health warnings conveniently covering the grubbiness, is palpable. There are no winners here. The air of tedium covers the large table in front of the bench occupied by solicitors, gardaí and local reporters. The judge asks a young man whose cider-drinking translated to threatening and abusive behaviour if he would like to spend "three months in the cookie jar".

The young man declined but was reminded from the bench that there was in any event no room in the cookie jar. He was given a series of fines totalling over £1,000.

Under this plethora of relatively trivial offences, a very serious charge was up for consideration. The charge brought by the DPP for common assault and criminal damage against John Gilligan for an alleged attack on our murdered colleague Veronica Guerin last September. Gilligan was now hiding in Amsterdam so the reporters and photographers who turned up were bound to be disappointed.

The group were going to be let down on more than one count. Once before, I had stood in the same forecourt with you for a planned hearing of the case. There was an adjournment after the usual Saturday-night drunken brawlers and six-month traffic offenders had been dealt with. I could not understand how this case, which had implications for the fundamentals of democracy, had received such low priority. Gilligan has publicly acknowledged that he made threats to you. It was, he said, to frighten you off. He did not mean what he said.

When District Justice John Brophy eventually got to the case, it was stated by Supt Brendan Quinn that, given the circumstances in which the chief prosecution witness was now dead, the State were entering a *nolle prosequi*. The judge had no choice and noted that there could be no effective evidence heard because of the unusual circumstances. He then made a moving plea to journalists present not to desert the legacy left by Veronica Guerin. He attacked the activities of the drug barons and urged those present not to allow the criminals take away their rights and freedom – "be not afraid," he said. We all then observed a minute's silence.

In that time I reflected on the ironies of the justice system: for the injunction case brought by John Traynor against the *Sunday Independent* to prevent an article by you being published posthumously was upheld because of the absence of your sworn affidavit while in the assault case the presence of a statement by you was meaningless in your absence. This is an irony too hard to bear.

Outside the "courthouse" the army of journalists swapped notes. A despairing moment outside a desolate rural place of justice where the timid face the music and the arrogant walk free. I never felt so low, in the face of such a pathetic postscript to a case that meant more than a million pounds and life to Veronica Guerin. There was one consolation: you would have been surprised and delighted with the solidarity of your comrades and the certain knowledge that the final chapter had yet to be written.

I am shot through, gripped by confusion and haunted by paranoia. There are so many holes in my psyche that

I might well have been pumped by a shadow figure. But I am alive and there's the rub because I feel dead, useless, incapable of doing anything meaningful.

I contemplate his photograph – his humiliation will not be complete until he confesses – which he will. Your killer can only choke on his own justice.

The pond out the back is dull. Underneath the murky waters I see the black outline of the fish, lying like silent submarines – no flies on the surface. The chestnut-tree has cast its autumn foliage to form a brown carpet over the grass. The ducks have gone somewhere even beyond the comprehension of Holden Caulfield.

I feel useless, lost, at once overpowered by nature's beauty and the base cruelty of man. Like Jesus and Socrates, you died for your beliefs and your message will not be in vain. And at least I was left with the task of taking that message to the world in celluloid form.

"Adieu, adieu, adieu remember me."

On my prophetic soul, I swear, Veronica, you will never be forgotten.

June 1997 approaches, it is a month to your first anniversary. The sun washes over the park, as hot as last year. The fish lie in a convoy below the surface of the pond. Below and beyond the chestnut the green landscape is mottled with brightly dressed teenagers, chattering like a dawn chorus, shirted business types on lunch-break, couples young and in love, older ones with children, the edge of their passion dulled by the practicalities of cohabiting, and older people in the autumn of their lives. They all glow in the sunshine with vigour, with life, but who knows what the future will bring?

"Like as the waves make towards the pebbled shore,
So do our minutes hasten to their end."

Life is short and it is all relative, all our time will come but right now that fact provides scant consolation. Our heroine is dead, long live the heroine.

My eye is distracted as usual by the jewels of light on the water which scatter my thoughts into the past and I trawl through the sea of memory.

Only weeks after you were laid to rest, American film companies began to contact me with offers. I listened with trepidation to their fucked-up material logic.

"You must call the main character 'Veronica'."

"I can't do that."

"Why not?"

"Because I promised her that I would not at her request."

"But she is dead."

"That does not remove my moral obligation to observe her wishes, it increases it."

There was a silence at the other end of the line.

Their lack of sensitivity was appalling. American film people think that they can buy anything and anybody by waving a cheque.

Some months before I had bumped into Richard Harris on Grafton Street and we adjourned for a few pints with a friend of his and my friend the ex-*Clannad* composer Pól Brennan. Harris is enthralling company, you'd love him. At the end of regaling us with his incomparable storytelling talents, he warned us never to compromise the integrity of the project by accepting money offers.

"They'll take your script and make shit of it, and there won't be a thing you can do," he said.

I remembered his and your words as one by one I rejected their approaches. In my mind I measured everything by what you would have wanted and that would always be my yardstick; neither of us was in this for the money. When I offered you the first instalment, a cheque for your storyline consultancy, you told me that the money did not interest you in any way. I remarked jokingly that you must be earning a fortune in the *Sunday Independent*.

"Shite," you said. "The phone was nearly cut off last week."

"Well," I said, "you have no excuse – take it."

You did reluctantly and I know in my heart that you were never motivated by the material things in this life. Truth motivated you, integrity was simply part of your nature and you wanted justice, a glimpse of heaven from the hell that Dublin had descended into. In fact, it was the vast wealth gained on the back of the unlimited spread of drugs that appalled you – greed and avarice you hated. Money could never entice, seduce or corrupt Veronica Guerin.

Saints don't go around saying *"go and shite"*, *"fuckin nonsense"* and *"jaysus"*. But if there was ever anyone I knew in this life that approached the description "divine creature" it is you. The divine springs from the pure spark of your soul. I hear you loud and clear from your heavenly byre: *"Mick, go and shite."*

But I'll go on, as you did when we sat opposite each other in the café – your eyes sparkling, righteous, fire burning in your heart. As one of your police sources Detective Gerry O'Carroll put it – "A slip of a girl with the heart of a lion."

Most of us are preoccupied by what we need and what is lacking in our lives. Through a time warp we bring Socrates window-shopping in Grafton Street with Veronica Guerin – outside Brown Thomas, packed with exotic wares and simultaneously observing *"What a lot of things I don't need"*.

In terms of indulgence, your chariot of fire brings you to your sources and destinations very speedily. But you don't wear the car like others do, flaunting the status like others do. It fitted like a glove. Never from the first time I travelled in it did I ever register the slightest hint of ostentation.

Why do I keep equating you with Socrates? While you had a clear philosophy, you were not a philosopher in the classical sense but you certainly did measure what you knew by what you did not know.

You took journalism in a different direction, just as Socrates changed the course of philosophy. And you were both prepared to die for what you believed in. There are very few of us, putting hand on heart, could say that. And both of you shared the description "enigmatic" and the role of messenger of the gods.

It has been said of the Greek philosopher that "You can seek him in the present, you can seek him in the past, but you can never find his equal".

I firmly believe that this is true in your case – it is not just that there will never be another Veronica Guerin but your like will never be seen again and no one can ever fill your shoes. Just yesterday the same man who christened you "the slip of a girl with the heart of a lion" said this very thing: "There is only one Veronica". And this is a man who is a poet, storyteller and philosopher as well as a superb policeman and a human who values integrity above the power of position and the drug of wealth.

And of course other journalists whose lazy and inept work methods were exposed. Veronica Guerin was never the one to hide behind a telephone in the newsroom. They called you naive, irresponsible, even dangerous. Of course, because they were too fuckin' lily-livered to do the same thing, so they had to knock it. Oh, this town of impotent begrudgers.

Like Brendan Behan, "fuck them" you would say. Believe this or not, they are still jealous and begrudging to this very day. They encourage myths about your motives and point to your death as some kind of spurious justification for their cowardly arguments.

Socrates inspired the same reaction from sections of Athenian society who had been stung by his philosophy. He, like you, was speaking for a power greater than himself but society could not recognise it. Socrates was threatened with death. He could have remained silent or backed off by pleading for lenience. He did not and you did not even after being threatened, shot and beaten. It takes an extraordinary person to stick by convictions in such circumstances.

For over 2000 years people have been asking why Socrates had to die and people will continue to ask why Veronica Guerin had to die. They challenged conventional perceptions of their respective societies and opposed injustice and corruption.

I walk down Northbrook Road cloistered by trees. The cherry blossom is in full bloom – such a beautiful sight, such evidence of the superior hand of nature. Can you see it, touch it? I pass by St. Anne's Hospital. In the early part of the last decade I held a woman's hand while during the height of the summer her life slipped away. We acknowledged the inevitable but the words death or dying never formed on our lips. She was a young beautiful woman and, because she did not fight her illness, I wondered had she a death wish or was there some dark secret that would remain buried up to and beyond her last breath. I looked at her ravaged body in the coffin before the lid was screwed on. I did not recognise this silent bag of bones. "She" had gone elsewhere.

Her passing had a profound effect on me. I brought her with me as I ran through the woods above Powerscourt Waterfall. I could see her reflection as my feet pounded through the watery tributaries of the river. I was suffused with unnatural strength and deep loneliness. For hours I floated through the grassy carpets of the woods and up the rocky inclines. Sweat cascaded from every pore of my body in rhythm with the waterfall.

Deep in my chest, the heart engine pumped relentlessly but I was a ghost and my body was immune to any physical stress or strain. The unexpected impact of this death of a woman I was not particularly close to in life drove me to face a challenge in which the genes of my Uncle Gus played their part. Myself and a group of like-minded people, including a mother and daughter, drove ourselves to the physical limits in Ireland's first full-length triathlon in the cause of alleviating the suffering of those dying from cancer. It was part exorcism but the demon of that death has never left me.

I pass through the gates into the park and I know that as soon as the green blades of grass grow I will receive guidance in this challenge. When I got home I got a phone call from one of your police contacts who invited me to Sundrive Garda Station where a party was being held to celebrate his promotion. It was a great night but in a conversation with him and another of the leading investigators into your murder, it emerged that they also felt a guiding hand and regularly placed their hands on the picture of you that has graced the walls of Lucan Garda Station since that fateful day in June 1996. And in the operations room in Lucan, the headquarters of the murder investigation, the lights still burn since the moment they were switched on over three years ago. The officers say they will remain on until the last gang member is brought to justice.

All held you in the highest regard and recognised the exceptional nature of your talent and dedication. None of these highly trained policemen ever hinted that Veronica Guerin was naive. After all, the most violent and sophisticated criminal organisation in the world, the American Mafia, had two golden rules – they could not kill journalists or cops. These policemen have pursued the perpetrators of the most heinous crime in Irish history with relentless skill and determination and with a degree of success that they readily admit has the trace of divine intervention.

Never in the relatively short history of organised crime, which the politicians now recognise as a bigger threat to Irish society than paramilitary activities, has there been such successful counteraction by the forces of law and order. The Criminal Assets Bureau have seized the assets of major crime barons and daily there are police busts of huge amounts of drugs. It should never be forgotten that the victories are all down to the life and death of one woman.

These things occupy my mind on a daily basis and sometimes I think I am in the midst of a mental labyrinth in which I have lost my way. But then I turn a corner and the path runs straight towards a tunnel of light. I can see clearly forever until I turn the next corner of doubt.

Yesterday I was in a corridor outside Court 6 of the District Court. I get talking to a detective. He knows a mutual source and he describes how he is going through the motions – doing the job but has no intention of sacrificing his health, family for the greater good of fighting crime. I accept his view – who gets a medal for commitment and dedication? As part of my research into violence and its effects I read a report chronicling the experience of policemen who have engaged in gun battles in which they have shot someone or been shot.

Each side of this terrible coin carries a nightmarish face – unless the perpetrator is psychopathic or pure scum it is difficult not to be traumatised by the shooting of another human. And nobody, not even in those categories, can escape deep disturbance by being shot. What emerged very clearly from this report was the lack of real support for the victims from the higher echelons of the force – in some instances a guard who shot a criminal felt on trial in the immediate aftermath – the regulation investigation of the incident added to the post-traumatic stress.

In one case a policeman who had been shot was in hospital. An hour after he had been admitted, a nurse came in and told him that the station was on, enquiring where his walkie-talkie was. "They have little to do," the nurse observed. I thought of all this as I talked to the detective. Your name came up in conversation. "Veronica Guerin, now there was a woman built of greater stuff. She would have never taken the view of her job that I do of mine. I know she made the ultimate sacrifice but she also made the ultimate difference. It was not in her to back off – the greater the intimidation, the bigger and more courageous her response."

This simple assessment from a man who recognised that he was in another category led me on to other explanations of your superior courage. You could never be happy if you acted against your better judgement – and what was the point of being unhappy? I can honestly say that I never met anyone who was more happy doing a job.

Your happiness and dedication led you to forget the ordinary practicalities of life – telephone bills, any bills, especially parking fines. I knew about the telephone, I had heard third-hand about the time that you ended up in a cell in Coolock with Cathal for non-payment of a fine. Both of you having a great laugh. Myth? Perhaps but it sounds characteristic. But the extent of it I only discovered at the bash in Sundrive Road and I dare to say I had a good laugh – only Veronica could have landed in this predicament. A jolly, extraordinarily tall policewoman of your acquaintance told me how she was instrumental in keeping you out of Mountjoy jail. For what offence? Clocking up a total of £2,500 in unpaid parking tickets. Your police friend giggled at the thought but then she reminded me that it was a serious situation. I could imagine our country's most accomplished investigative reporter being led through the gates of Mountjoy Prison for not paying parking fines.

It was close, you were that close. Jesus, when I think of it, the woman in the sharp suit clutching the mobile, being led from her red chariot to reside in the Victorian poverty of the jail slum in Phibsborough – and I know you would have made it into an event – Veronica Guerin – Mountjoy Prison – the Inside Story. But in the end what has that knowledge and the search for truth and justice and exposure of corruption got to do with parking fines? You could be more than forgiven for leaving behind the practicalities of everyday living in the rush. You are not alone.

It is a dark, rainy and windy Friday afternoon in February 1997. I am in the offices of *Irish Screen*, the company which is developing the script. The producer, Nigel Warren Green, the casting director John Hubbard in London and I are due to have a conference call with a Hollywood agent and his client, an actress whom we are trying to attract to the main part of the Journalist. The actress has been sitting on the fence and so we are determined to force the position so that we can move on to look for another actor to take the part. Ros Hubbard, John's partner, has sent a fax to the Hollywood agent warning that if the conference call does not take place at the time arranged, we reserve the right to look elsewhere.

Nigel receives a call from a Hollywood manager by the name of Carol Bodie. Her client, Winona Ryder, has read the script and wants the part. We can hardly disguise our shock and surprise and delight – but we must await the conference call. Carol Bodie rings back – dump this actress and you have Winona.

We have come a long way from our innocent

consultations in Café Java. I have seen Winona recently in *The Crucible* and she delivers a brilliant gritty performance that unfortunately escaped public notice in one of those ironies that puts a high-class film like this in the turkey category. But it convinces me in retrospect, since we had not approached her, she fits that essential description – a slip of a girl with the heart of a lion. We are not trying to replicate Veronica Guerin but to recreate her spirit. Of all the Hollywood "A" list actors this is one – a real actor as opposed to simply a pretty face.

I leave the office about 7pm and join the throngs in Maguire's Pub in Baggot Street. A half an hour later Nigel appears and motions me to go outside. I think there is something wrong. "I have just spoken to Winona," he said. "She said that she has waited all her life to play this part. She swears that she will not let us down – she is doing it for Veronica."

I am amazed and thrilled because of the basic level of commitment – this is not just another actress wanting to do a part – Winona Ryder's motivation is informed by something and possibly someone else. Right then I had no clue who or what but later on it would be revealed in a fashion.

We get on with the dull mechanics of putting a film together with the knowledge that it might never happen. There is so much mystique about this business; getting a project of this nature together is like climbing Everest naked and handcuffed. There are legalities, strategies, financial plans and worst of all a plethora of opinions (generally conflicting) about the way forward. Where is the art in all this, I ask myself – there is talk of budgets, schedules, cast, crew – it feels like the story has got left behind in the rush.

By its nature, film is a collaborative medium, but, believe me, your patience is regularly and sorely tried. You are taught very quickly to swallow your pride, practically on a daily basis. It would be very easy to get pissed off but the first learning curve is to keep the head and bite the tongue. It is my business to maintain the integrity of the story which we had forged in outline and take on all comers who lay claim to the trophy entitled *I Know Everything*.

You have come across the same thing in journalism but it is only in the halfpenny place. The similarity is in the area of ego, a territory in which neither of us could be described as modest. You have had attacks on your work and *modus operandi* on many occasions, it won't surprise you that it is still going on but the film equivalent of the article, the script, is subjected to analysis and treatment more common to the butcher's slab.

Like a prime piece of beef, it is greeted with great enthusiasm at first. But then the knife is sharpened, the artistic bone shattered and the fat mercilessly trimmed. Could you blame the writers for an odd squeal? We were yet to encounter the Hollywood studio reader who has one hour flat to digest the story and probably half that to deliver a damning judgement. The reader is either a failed scriptwriter or a wannabe – the animal does not get even the most minuscule credit – thus it would hardly be logical to expect compliments – another bigger more efficient slab – this time closer to the mortuary variety.

I remember you telling me a story about covering a

murder investigation in which the spouse was the chief suspect for the killing of her husband. As you approached her she literally spat the words at you: "A prostitute wouldn't do your job."

Well, we were both aware that journalism was considered a whore's profession and ironically discovered that this description was equally apt for the scriptwriter – everyone (in a metaphorical sense) gets to fuck the writer – the producers, the lawyers, the financiers, the director and the actors. Comforting thought – the agonies of journalism are great, the impaling of the scriptwriter somewhat more complete. As David Mamet puts it so eloquently – "for the writer, film is a collaborative medium – bend over".

I digress. Not that I want to turn all this into a whine but I do remember at our meetings in Café Java the odd pleasure of a good bitching session.

People will try to deconstruct the importance of the unprecedented impact of Veronica Guerin's work, as they will and already have done to our collaboration. Whether they are to be more pitied than despised, I know what your reaction would be – instant and devastating. You were once criticised by a well-known pundit with a large mouth for not condemning the Provisional IRA. You rang him immediately and had in the inimitable phrase "his guts for garters". The apology was forthcoming. So the deconstructors had better beware.

Returning to the celluloid whore's profession and the lows it engenders as well as the highs, I received great consolation while reading a biography of the great crime writer Raymond Chandler. He had been subjected to iniquities of the system while spending an albeit lucrative period as a Hollywood writer. He offered this prescription for its ills:

"What Hollywood seems to want is a writer who is ready to commit suicide at every story conference. What it actually gets is the fellow who screams like a stallion in heat and then cuts his throat with a banana. The scream demonstrates the artistic purity of his soul and he can eat the banana while somebody is answering a telephone call about some other picture."

A parallel: I remember the time you interviewed the Monk at your house for 6 hours. Your exclusive ran to something approaching 2,500 words but the article when printed ran to around a 1,000. You went berserk. Executive in charge thought your piece was "too soft" on the subject. You got your way – the article ran in full the following week. Could anyone accuse you of not being a persuasive woman?

These tribulations seem all the more galling when one considers that we shared the process in September of 1995 through the shock, horror and trauma of your death to the eve of your anniversary. But the pain is trivial when compared to what Graham, Cathal, your family, colleagues and the nation endured. I have dedicated this book to all those people. The land has been so dark and wet for the last week as if nature reflected on the anniversary approaching and the heavens wept openly. The sky is one mass of angry black threatening cloud hanging overhead like a frayed dirty carpet.

The misery is apt and reminds me of Keats' opening verse of spiritual loss and longing in "La Belle Dame Sans Merci" –

"And this is why I sojourn here
Alone and palely loitering,
Though the sedge is wither'd from the lake,
And no birds sing."

There are times when I question what I am doing and get overtaken by self-doubt. We never had much difficulty in this department, it was as close as you get to a perfect understanding. But I know there are people who will misconstrue what my colleagues and I are doing – we are attempting to profit from a tragedy or exploit a good story. It doesn't matter a damn that you and I were working on this and had come to a clear agreement about what the story was going to be in essence.

Let them go and fuck themselves, you would say, and sometimes I can take on that skin but other times I am simply astounded how humans, fellow Dubliners at that, can slither so low they render the snake a contender for the Olympic high jump title.

Listen to this. A month ago myself and Nigel are in Los Angeles to meet Winona and her manager Carol Bodie. LA is a town of posers, fast talkers and transparent film types, all pitching like hell and talking pure shite – but great to be a somewhat impartial observer in Tinsel Town. We meet Winona and Carol who are the antithesis of the Hollywood Stereotypes – you would love them – Winona is utterly genuine, intelligent and committed totally to a project which both has your mark and will be dedicated to your memory. In fact an astrologer has read her chart and traced this role back to her birth. Is this bullshit? If it is everyone is allowed their quota. Personally I have as much respect for astrology as crystal balls. Fate is beyond the reach of limited human understanding.

We cement the relationship established on the phone, just as you and I did. I recognise a look in Winona's eye which you had – the focused eye, the mirror of someone who wants to change people's perception of something really basic about life. She is on the one road with you. We all have a clear understanding about where we are going.

We part with the same hug, the same purity of heart. I am so happy for this project – for her, for you. The next day Nigel meets Carol to create a business bond. This works really well; after a two-hour meeting, it is clear they are on the same wavelength. Carol tells Nigel that she has checked us out and we come out one hundred per cent. But, and there always seems to be a but – she would like to be totally open – calls have been made to her office, rubbishing *Irish Screen*, Nigel Warren Green and Michael Sheridan. Nigel, in his usual polite tone enquires the source of these calls – naturally he doesn't want to know the identity of the callers. At least he says he doesn't, knowing I would give my eye-teeth for them – I am a bit closer to your nature in that regard.

"Dublin," Carol replies. He is gobsmacked.

Later, when he relates this information, my blood bubbles and I see red in three dimensions.

"Fuck the begrudgers," says Nigel.

"Yeah, I would," I reply, "with a specially designed nutcracker with added spices."

There is no use asking Veronica Guerin would she believe that.

Talk to me, you would say, and I am talking. Does all this hurt? Whether it does or not, the real trick is not letting it get to one, even to the extent of pretending it doesn't hurt. We all hurt easily and that is the truth of it. You would not have reacted to the pundit the way you did had he not touched a vulnerable chord and that is totally understandable. The so-called tough person is simply the one that manages to hide the vulnerable side more successfully. But it is surprisingly easy to reduce arrogance to a pathetic whimper. To exist in life and to work to a goal is difficult enough without considering oneself humiliated. We all get on with it, not very easily it has to be said.

But all this has to be put into perspective by a matter of life and death and an event which reduces those petty prejudices and frail posturing to their precise importance. This is Thursday, June 26, 1997 – the first anniversary of the slaying of a heroine.

All this morning there are tributes to you on the news and the RTE news magazine programme hosted by Pat Kenny did a particularly good job with assessments by friends and colleagues. Despite the great strides taken against the criminal underworld since last year I get the feeling that you have left a huge vacuum – obviously personally but also professionally. There are excellent crime reporters in this city but there will never be another Veronica Guerin.

Like Hillary on Everest, you scaled the heights where nobody would take the mountain on and now everyone else can only aspire to palely shadow your footsteps. There is, of course, a lot of knowledge with hindsight but most observers admit that no one but you had a hint of the extent of the Warehouseman's empire or the structure of his criminal hierarchy or the depth of his connections with the INLA. There is mention of Judas whose role is only now known in its completeness. He is suffering from some pangs of conscience and is racked with fear. He is being picked off the floor of a Spanish pub every night.

There have been facile remarks today made along the easy categorisation of the good, the bad and the ugly. The distinction is too glib, a mite superficial. What you were dealing with was evil in its most dangerous and naked guise. My father Martin was always a firm believer in the reality of evil, the appearance of the devil in man, in the present – not to mind the afterlife. My mother Patsy, a woman of the world, of deep intelligence, liberal leanings and socialist politics combined with a Christian faith, concurred. My irreligious inclinations took some argument but when it was presented it was simple as all truths ultimately are. Anyone who contemplated the horrors of the Second World War and most particularly the Holocaust would find it hard to deny that perpetrators of the greatest crimes against mankind were proof of the manifestation of evil.

The images of Belsen, the mounds of bodies astride a vast open grave, each human in a crazy contorted position, the ovens full of ashes and bones and the horde of dazed inmates, starved and gaunt, staring from behind barbed wire provide more than ample evidence of the horrific power of evil.

That evil was alive and well and thriving in Dublin and it took a slip of a girl with a lion heart to recognise it and take it on. And remember what a master of disguise the spirit of evil is – how long it took the world to discover the genocide perpetrated by Hitler.

Miraculously the sun bursts forth from behind the clouds. I can see it from where I write – the mezzanine café in Bewleys. Grafton Street is like a flowerbed made of people. The brief hint of summer makes the girls glow and spreads a light of optimism over the crowded thoroughfare. I walk later towards Stephen's Green, floating invisibly among the throng. A string quartet of music students play my favourite passage from Vivaldi's Four Seasons. The music is poignant and lays a heavy hand on my heart. The tree-tops sway gently over the magisterial entrance to the jewel of all Dublin parks.

But today it seems to me a painted backdrop to an opera or ballet – the swan that floats in the centre of the pond with the tea-house in the background is transformed to the frozen image of still life. I experience the presence of people in the distance like the shadowy figures on a Caravaggio canvas. Birdsong is a distant sound-effect like the chiming of an offstage bell or the distant peal that woke one as a child who wondered what this toll in a far-off field meant – doom or sanctuary? Somewhere I hear the frenetic cackling alarm-call of a disturbed magpie. It is amazing how purely symphonic on one hand and how cacophonous on the other, the singing of our feathered friends can be.

All along the perimeter of the green there hangs a vast exhibition of amateur paintings. I glance in the direction of a pastoral scene but it seems even less significant than the real thing. I admire but can feel no empathy with the work of the artist.

I walk towards the Shelbourne Hotel. A girl walks ahead of me, her hair glistening in the sunshine, her hands full of newly acquired shopping. I wonder what disaster will befall her in the future – because none of us are free of it.

The side bar of the Shelbourne is hot and sweaty.

Smoke from cigars and cigarettes drifts nonchalantly as a cloud through the brilliant shaft of sunlight pouring through the Kildare Street window. I am surrounded by the magpie-toned roar of country accents, "culchies" to you Veronica, who are frenetically discussing the formation of our new Government which is taking place just yards away in the Dáil. Oh, what petty ambitions are harboured by this bunch of spruced-up gombeen men intent on shoving their crude political philosophy down the necks of the suspecting public! Don't they remember what day this is?

I drink a beer, it might as well be a pint of urine. Ger comes in. We remember this time last year – I have a flashback to her waterfall – now there are no tracks of her tears. We remember but in truth we want to forget – not you, but that awful moment and that ghastly emotional paralysis – there is hardly a person that does not want to wave bereavement goodbye. I don't want to get cynical but when I think of those monkeys in suits down in the Dáil lining up for the historic photograph – a longshot, of course, because the cameraman cannot enhance such a fine representative body of Irish manhood – I want to puke.

There is a man near us who was former head of a banking group who was kidnapped by the General's gang. He keeps glancing in my direction – who the fuck does he think I am? A journalist? I am in foul humour – I'm going to confess to you – I want this day to pass. I feel like a punctured tyre and full of guilt for my emotional impotence.

We go to our local O'Briens. It is packed and noisy. What have these people, noisy and loud, got to be so happy about? Their voices fade into the brown wood panelling. I can't get drunk – I won't get drunk. Later I stare into a plate of cannelloni, I could be happily eating cement.

I lay back in the bed embraced by the darkness. I wonder what it is to be alive and guess what it is like to be dead. *"Imagine Dead Imagine."* I can't. I'm an awful fool, Veronica, I know it – but a sad one. We miss you a lot.

While the vicissitudes of the film roll inexorably on and we complete a fifth draft, I live in a sort of a limbo and the energy I devote to this letter is transferred to another medium, not as intimate but no less direct. I sometimes feel guilty that I am not addressing you in the second but the third person and wrestle to get the truth and balance of the story right.

In the script I have to be that bit more distant and attempt to distil that huge amount of information gathered with and about Veronica Guerin. It is getting close to two years since we began to collaborate. It seems a lifetime, because for hardly a day have I let slip our target. From being centre-stage in your life and immediately after your death, your name crops up as a oblique reference in trials involving members of the assassin gang.

The Warehouseman (John Gilligan), is incarcerated in Belmarsh high-security prison in London and proceedings for his extradition to face the charge of murdering Veronica Guerin, importing several tons of cannabis, and having firearms, has got under way. Another charge of possessing laundered money in Heathrow Airport, the site of his original arrest, is to be postponed. Gilligan is in a bind and will do everything to delay facing the music, including an appeal to the House of Lords. But the leading investigators of the Irish Police force believe that it is certain he will be brought back to face the music. Another member of the gang, Paul Ward, who is alleged to have disposed of the gun and the motorbike has been in custody since October of last year and will also face a murder charge but, like the rest, will fight all the way to the Supreme Court to try to get his trial quashed. Two other members of the gang, Russell Warren and Charles Bowden, are turning State's evidence in the trials and are part of the first witness-protection programme in the history of the State. Great strides have been taken in the fight against the crime and drug barons – the Criminal Assets Bureau established in the wake of your death has seized a huge amount of cash and property belonging to the godfathers.

We all find this heartening but it took your sacrifice to concentrate the will of the State. Thus the plain prose of newspaper reports in which your name is prominently displayed is upsetting and so much more for your family, the constant and unrelenting reminders in the newspapers and on radio and television.

I find this disturbing when I should know that as a journalist this is normal practice. But then I know you and that makes it different – we all want to write the story, not be a subject of the news. But it happens – remember our colleagues who died after a light plane on a Beaujolais promotion crashed on the way to France?

Well, that was shocking but this is different. Nothing goes away from me as I search for a perspective, a meaning, a resolution. Even the passage of time reveals little except an easing on the gut and a lift of the heaviness in my heart. But the sorrow never ends.

I see a picture of your killer in the paper – he is being remanded on an unrelated charge. He has dyed what little hair rests on the sides of his head black. What is going on in his head? What sense of perverted vanity resides there? Does the mirror not tell him the truth or does he treat it as he does the confessional?

My abhorrence of his existence does not preclude a certain sense of curiosity. I'd like, genuinely like, to understand what makes this excuse for humanity tick. I'd like to look into the eye of a man who kills a human being mercilessly and then runs and hides from the responsibility in the darkness of the confessional. In a revenge fantasy, I am the priest and when he asks for absolution, I remove the grille, loop his throat with cheesewire and with the words "Absolution? Take it out of this" despatch him to his Maker to face the only trial that really matters. Perhaps I would say "Blood of Christ" as his yellow blood spilled to the floor. Bad thoughts? Certainly, isn't that what grieving is all about? And we all want to see justice done without the law's delay. I remember the words of the detective who questioned this man – "I would not find it in myself to harbour hatred for him."

Perhaps there is something in that but how would that killer feel if a member of his family was despatched as mercilessly? His wife, for example? Would he contemplate revenge?

On the radio this morning a pundit is bleating about the media exaggerating the level of crime in the country. His bullshit makes my flesh creep. It gets worse. The interviewer points out the explanation for the drop as the sweeping measures introduced in the wake of the murder of a journalist. "Veronica Guerin wasn't murdered for her reporting," the pundit counters.

No, she got shot, beaten and murdered because she was out picking daisies where she shouldn't have been. You would have picked up the phone immediately and gutted the blind pundit. So blind, that two days after his "assessment" there were a further four murder investigations under way. A couple of days previously two cops had the shit beaten out of them in the Temple Bar area. The English lager louts are just part of the problem.

God, Veronica, you were so different, so refreshing, such an inspiration – the whole journalistic scene seems as flat and stale as last Christmas's fart. It's either cheap and nasty or plain boring.

I wander lonely as a cloud through St Stephen's Green. It's sort of a delicious feeling treading this familiar path without knowing a single soul. It seems like the city is a million miles away. I can hear the traffic like the distant roar of thunder. The sun has settled like a golden blanket on the green grass. In the pond the swan floats, gracefully, idly like a yacht in Antibes harbour. The ducks fight over sodden pieces of abandoned bread. Children fuss over them but the feathered friends are spoilt and ignore them. Couples lie entwined, caught frozen in the eternity of a lazy Saturday afternoon. No intimations of mortality for the young in love. Unfortunately, I remember over two decades ago, but those days are gone forever – I should just let them go.

I pass by the fountain of Phalli gaily pissing water skywards. I see the flags of the Shelbourne Hotel through the trees on the park's perimeter. I remember, as a child, on this very spot meeting a garrulous, rough, bloated-looking man in the presence of my father Martin who communicated with this dishevelled man *as Gaeilge*. They parted and later at the end of Grafton Street he conversed with another man in the same language – which happens to be my native tongue, alas lost.

This man had dyed black hair with a polished sheen and his face was caked with a yellow powder. He moved his hands like a mime artist and his lips were constantly pouted as if about to kiss. We moved on into Westmoreland Street and again my father stopped under the *Irish Times* clock.

This time the man was squat with dark bushy eyebrows which protruded from under a black hat. They talked in whispered tones in a language which was familiar but beyond my childish grasp. Later my father told me I should remember this trio. The first man was Brendan Behan, the second Michael MacLiammoir and the third Flann Ó Briain.

That was Dublin in the much-quoted innocent and rare old times when neighbours left the keys in the door and helped each other to tea, butter and sugar when short. As in Pete St John's song.

> *"Ring a ring a rosy,*
> *As the light declines,*
> *I remember Dublin City*
> *In the rare ould times."*

Well, so they say, and maybe you remember something of the latter part of that era. Despite the stink of degradation and corruption, there is still an echo of that spirit left in the oul home town. That day, for example, in St. Stephen's Green, I met nobody, but soon I would and perhaps experience some shadow of a Joycean epiphany.

And so it was. I was drawn as usual to the excellent bar at the side of that august establishment that flew the flags. And there I met purely by chance a girl-friend of yours. We talked and talked about media. What else? At this stage, I did not realise that there was any connection between her and you.

She enquired about the film project, the working relationships involved and the sensitivities of the issues involved. I explained the background, the time we had spent together and the eventual goal that was set. It must have inspired some measure of trust because she opened up and began to talk about your fun-loving traits, the generosity of spirit and the great relationship you had with Graham and Cathal, all of which in a short space I had recognised instinctively and had confirmed – it was the character I had recognised, one which despite its greatness did not attract sycophants because they would have been recognised and instantly banished. But there was something I did not know which was about to be revealed. The blonde attractive woman looked at me and paused for a couple of beats. "I probably shouldn't be telling you this but I will. *Veronica had cancer.*"

I had heard some unsubstantiated rumour but dismissed it at the time. I was shocked. I had rarely met a human being with so much energy and vivacity – with a life-threatening illness? Surely not. Your friend went on to explain that you had had extensive treatment including chemotherapy and the cancer had receded. Your friend said that you had kept the illness a very close secret even from your own family. You didn't want any sympathy or fuss, you just wanted to get on with your life and work, this was not going to be a handicap. I wondered if the intimation of mortality had anything to do with your drive or motivation but I concluded that those were always your strong characteristics before, illness may have given you an extra impetus. My mind flashed back to the woman I had watched die in St Anne's Hospital. I had written extensively about the disease in the wake of that traumatic experience. I asked the type. Lymph cancer, she replied. I was speechless. The exact same kind as the woman who had lasted just a year. Lymphoma, a cancer of the secondary blood system.

August could have been a wicked month for us but it was avoided by a simple twist of fate. The fifth draft of the script has been given total approval by the American Executive Producer Peter Newman, his partners Greg Johnston and Ira Deutchman, the former head of New Line, a powerful independent features outfit. That's the good news.

The bad is that Winona Ryder, who was cool on the fourth draft, has not yet given a reaction, but we all agree that because the script has brought the central character closer to you she may not play the part.

Her reticence has been on the Hollywood grapevine and the agent representing another bankable actress has made an approach on behalf of his client but we cannot entertain any real dialogue until Winona makes up her mind. But it is comforting to know that there is such attention at that high level.

I will be sorry to lose Winona with whom I believe I could establish a very fruitful artistic rapport – her talent has yet to make its true mark. But I accept that if it is not to be then there is a good reason – there is a time for every purpose under Heaven.

This does not look like being a season of mist and mellow fruitfulness. The gathering swallows I eye with a sense of foreboding – not simply for the now escalating approach of winter, but the normal pessimism associated with film projects – is this ever going to happen?

It is closing on two years since we began this collaboration and so much muddy water has flowed under the bridge that there are times when, not seized by a fire to complete this mission, I am gripped by a mixture of apathy and melancholy.

This is probably exacerbated by the fact that I am no longer among my journalistic colleagues, having been working on the script and associated matters full-time since last April. I know that you worked on your own most of the time but you had the companionship of contacts and constant communication with the people you worked closest to in the *Sunday Independent*.

Whatever faults media people have and there are many, I can't imagine many professionals share the same sense of camaraderie. Some of the critics will say – what is he talking about? But then the cynics don't recognise what we often talked about.

I know you'd understand because there was never a trace of cynicism evident during any of our conversations, which frequently veered towards journalism and, to be fair, good honest gossip. And you often expressed appreciation of the valued backing of colleagues at all levels of journalism. You were relatively new to journalism and there was no time for disillusion to set in; you were a privileged being because of your personality and the quality of your work, who never had to kowtow or lick anyone's arse or curry favour. A lot of that goes on – in every walk of life and it takes a unique person to avoid becoming a courtier.

There is an art in journalism in spite of the intense profit motive that drives newspaper managements. Most journalists of our acquaintance are not driven by money because the fact is that rich journalists are a rarity.

Film is somewhat different. There are few people involved in the film industry who are not motivated by the thought of the huge rewards that success in the medium brings. The fact that so few people relative to the size of the industry reach those heights does not affect this motivation. It is possible to be a highly successful journalist and penurious. Even the most profligate of successful film makers or actors would find it hard to piss all the money down the drain.

Dennis Hopper, famed for his outrageous appetite for drugs and bad living and a long spell exiled from main-street Hollywood, still managed to build up a priceless art collection.

I know of one Dublin journalist with a similar appetite for drink and a talent approaching genius. He has never drunk or toiled far from the yawn of the gutter.

In film everything has its price and real talent or the search for truth is low on the list of priorities. I had a raging row with a producer recently because the sole thrust of his conversation was money, how much he had spent on this project, how his company could not "subsidise" arty types forever, how there was no guarantee that he would get his money back – pounds, shillings and pence – no mention of the integrity or the quality of the project or the huge effort of research and

117

torturous writing that is involved in the simplest of scripts, not to mind a complex subject. I raged and ranted and took the door from the hinges as I left the room. I know you would have done the same. But in a way I am lucky because the majority of the producers do not think this way, and believe me, I appreciate them because they are a rarity in the business. In time he would appreciate the real value of the project.

Winona Ryder decides not to play the main part, her management do not explain exactly why but they are magnanimous and leave the door open for involvement in other projects *Irish Screen* here and *Redeemable in America* might have in the future.

When a major actress pulls out of a film, the project often collapses because the premise of all financing rests with the attachment of a box-office draw. But the parameters of this film have been firmly set down and accepted by all sides – the story is bigger than any individual. So there is no disappointment in a large sense. The script is immediately sent to the agent of Frances McDormand, the Oscar-winning star of *Fargo*, who already approached Peter Newman and Nigel Warren Green at the New York premiere of *Mrs Brown*. The agent loves the script and is most anxious for his client to play the main part.

For our part, Frances is more mature and therefore more suitable for the part in the new script. She has won an Oscar and therefore her attraction at the box office is more than matched by her credibility as an actress. But she is busy on another project and will not be able to read the script for another 10 days. Everyone is confident she will like it but who knows?

I had a meeting with John and Ros Hubbard, the casting directors. With such credits behind them as *The Commitments* and *Evita* and a host of other quality vehicles, they are the most down-to-earth couple, full of wit and laughter. We discuss a list of major actresses we could approach if Frances doesn't work out. You would be flattered at some of the names.

I'm a first-time feature-film director – what would they want to work for me for? The story is bigger than all of us, the Hubbards remind me. Yes but so is the incremental responsibility. There are times when I wonder if I am able for the huge demands that will be put on me during the shoot – no proper sleep for 10 weeks, long, long days, lots of pressures and lots of problems – everyone coming at me from every direction. I shudder at the thought – it fills me full of fear and melancholy.

And then I think of my petty worries and compare them to what you did – sacrificed your life for justice – how pathetic are my little obsessions. I'll remember you as the morning rose. This is your parting gift so I'd better be a proven curator to this monument. Do you understand how sometimes it is beyond me? Get on with it Mick, you'd say. So, in Beckett's words, I'll go on.

Meanwhile the net is closing on the bastards who organised your death. The Warehouseman is being extradited from London to face drug-trafficking charges and the murder of Veronica Guerin. Strangely it all seems too distant. Having immersed myself in the subject for so long, I am beginning to find it difficult to separate fact from fiction. Hardly a day passes that there isn't some reference to the gang in the newspapers, radio, television

– there is a mighty determination to have these people pay and crush their power.

September steals inexorably on through the pleasant clear light of an Indian Summer but I am reminded of the onset of winter by the gathering carpet of leaves in the park and the ghost of the cherry-blossom in Northbrook Road. The seasons hold up such an accurate mirror to life. Two years have passed since our first meeting – it seems a lifetime.

I sit in Café Java at the table, one side empty, forever. Through the window the business of the city is captured like one of the back-projected street scenes in a forties film. Cars pass through the S-bend southbound towards the Burlington Hotel, Donnybrook. A suited man rushes along the footpath, mobile phone implanted in his ear; students cycle nonchalantly towards the lecture halls; a young woman, power-dressed, walks haughtily and purposefully up her elevating career path. How many of these fleeting shadows of Dublin citizenry appreciate how immeasurably the quality of their lives have been improved by the absence in that chair opposite me?

There is no doubt in anyone's mind that the sacrifice that you made has been directly responsible for the defeat of the reign of terror, the incarceration of the main players in the most dangerous criminal gang that this country has ever known. Plus the dismantling of numerous criminal and drug-trafficking empires and ultimately the introduction of a new sense of security and safety for what Myles na Gopaleen referred to as the "plain people of Ireland".

My eyes watch the street and move like a tracking camera across to the pub at the corner, my local, O'Brien's, through the door and to the end of the outer bar. It is two weeks before. I am in the company of a detective inspector and his brother, a forensic psychiatrist, whose speciality is psychopaths.

Two mighty intelligent, articulate and excitable Kerrymen, they get even more excitable with drink. Your name comes up. The policeman is one of your most ardent admirers while his brother cannot understand why you could have put the pursuit of the criminals in front of the needs of your family or exposed yourself or them to danger and ultimately death.

It is a debate which does not allow for easy answers. It borders faith, courage, naiveté, foolhardiness, sheer bravery and a number of other imponderables. Did I know exactly what went on in your mind? Of course not. Certainly I had an acquaintance with your views and any writer's ability to sum up character – but there is a part of everyone's mind that not even the most intimate can gain entrance to. Ambiguity and contradiction are essential cogs in the wheel of existence and I agree with Empson that life involves maintaining oneself between contradictions that can't be solved by analysis and, as Beckett recognised, there is a deeper instinct than the mere animal instinct of self-preservation.

The question was posed: did you think that you were going to die? There is nothing complex about that question and I had discussed that possibility with you. But I could not answer it with any degree of absolute authority. The question is that there is hardly a person alive that has not asked that question of him or herself. But it is an imagining, a momentary fluctuation, a temporary paralysing thought like the reaction to a rat running across the rafters. The thought is usually dispatched as quickly as it comes for who would be a spectator at their own death? I turned to Freud for support. "Our death is indeed unimaginable and whenever we make the attempt to imagine it, we can perceive that we really survive as spectators." All the same many of us imagine ourselves as spectators looking on at our own funeral, but when we attend someone else's we are greeted by silence.

The argument went to and fro. History, observed the detective, is littered with examples of heroic figures like Veronica Guerin who eschewed every perceived comfort and value of their existence in the name of truth, freedom and justice. Courage, he said is the genesis of all other virtues. The psychiatrist conceded that courage is a quality by definition that defies logical behaviour. The mountaineer must be aware of the dangers of climbing but cannot be overwhelmed by the possibility of dying – otherwise there would be no mountaineers or patriots or radical thinkers or campaigning journalists. None of these people can afford to really believe that they are going to die. Of course they can conceive, as we all do, of the possibility. But even when confronted by the probability, as you were, you could not flinch.

Most people found this a mystery but there are the simplest examples of humans who face imminent death soberly and make friends with the necessity of dying. Suicides do (and the act – whatever the perceived morality – requires courage), as does the patient in the hospice, for there is only one exit from this place – in a box. Similarly the inhabitants of the old folks' home – death stares them in the face. Why aren't they screaming?

You know those arguments blown about in a hurricane of pints. No great conclusions, but the process is valuable and believe me it never stops. Veronica Guerin will never die in our hearts and minds.

I have been writing this epistle for a long time and I have always thought that the genesis was spiritual and thus I didn't question the motivation.

I got my answer in a Church of Ireland chapel in Zion Road, Rathgar at the wonderful October-lit funeral of a beautiful woman, Una Slott, whose soul, the essence of goodness, was taken away by a flight of angels some days ago. Behind the altar in gold ornate lettering, Christ's exhortation at the Last Supper – *Do this in Remembrance of Me*. In remembrance and in celebration and to unravel a meaning as mysterious as the Eucharist. And, as with Christ, your death has given us light that I humbly attempt to reflect.

While I was in Los Angeles, I bought a book by Sammy "the Bull" Gravano who turned state's evidence against his Mafia Boss, John Gotti, "the Teflon Don", who had for many years frustrated repeated efforts by the FBI to bring him to justice. The FBI eventually tracked down Gotti's headquarters, had it bugged and recorded hundreds of hours of tapes which chronicled the workings of the criminal of New York's *capo di capo*. Some years ago I read a book based on the operation. The Gotti Tapes provided a fascinating insight into organised crime but also into the mind of Gotti whose ruthless penchant for brutally murdering anyone who got in his megalomaniac way was blood-curdling.

In stature, if not in style, Gotti reminded me of the Warehouseman. Both small men with monstrous egos and degenerate appetites, revelling in their power and money and absolutely impervious to the consequence of their actions. They held human life, other than their own, in utter contempt and as disposable as the kitchen rubbish. Both ruled by fear. Terror, both inside and outside their empires, their most dangerous weapon.

I discussed the psychopathic mind with the detective for whom I had bought the book and with his brother, the psychiatrist. I had been under the illusion that a psychopath was a complex human being capable of horrible and complex behaviour. No, I was told – the psychopath is frighteningly simple – despite coming in various categories in terms of dangerous behaviour.

The psychopath, to use a computer analogy, can possess the same hard drive as the rest of us, but generally it is the software that is defective. That software is missing conscience, inhibition of violent impulse, understanding of consequence and any imprint of remorse. So killing, whether impulsive or planned, makes absolutely no impact on the perpetrator.

Gotti was such an animal as was the Warehouseman, who displayed this trait when he threatened to "kill you and your neighbours and ride your son" and when he beat you to a pulp outside his country residence. There is little doubt in the minds of the Special Branch men that pursued this assault case that this man would have beaten you to death if the circumstances were more favourable for the act.

To face the full wrath of a psychopath is the most nightmarish occurrence and a horrendous experience for even the most stout-hearted. The psychiatrist claimed that he could diagnose a psychopath in five minutes by looking into the eyes. He explained that the violence perpetrated by the psychopath is self-explained in the most stark and simple of terms: "They were wreckin' me head" is a common justification. Another characteristic is a determination, utter and single-minded, in achieving a goal no matter what the consequence.

John Gotti organised the assassination of the previous *capo di capo* of New York's Mafia, Paul Castellano, in broad daylight despite the potential consequence of the wiping out of himself, the gang and his own empire.

You were wreckin' the Warehouseman's head by your determination to pursue the assault case and he was willing to risk his empire too.

The immediate consequence of both their actions were at first different, but in time, the same self-destruct button had been pushed. And there was another chilling coincidence. Both Gotti and the Warehouseman's success at evading prosecution had been based on violent intimidation. When the Warehouseman told the detective that "he would never make it to Court", the threat rang, not hollowly, but utterly true. This intimidation which Gotti also practised was based on an invincible arrogance and a thought-process suffocated by the Elixir of Power. And what power is more absolute than that over life and death?

Even in this green pond on the periphery of Europe, the Warehouseman ran a business equal in turnover to the Beau Brummel of New York's Mafia. The stakes were that high that he shared Gotti's view – anyone who got in his way was going to be whacked. Sammy "the Bull" Gravano organised and carried out the "Teflon Don's" hits. We have already been introduced to the

Warehouseman's gunman, the bald-headed Holy Joe who professed in a weak moment to possessing a conscience.

The difference between him and Gravano was that when the chips came down, Sammy the Bull, confronted with his life's achievement of violent deeds, was horrified by what he had perpetrated in the name of the Mafia and Gotti and confessed and sought absolution by offering Gotti to the FBI, breaking the cardinal rule of the *Cosa Nostra* and putting his own life in mortal danger. He proved that he did not qualify as a psychopath because he showed remorse – even somewhat late, a conscience.

As did a member of the Warehouseman's gang, Charlie Bowden, who despite making £5,000 a week shifting drugs and guns was ultimately sickened by the cold-blooded murder of a woman journalist. He has turned his back on his mentor and is giving evidence against the biggest godfather of crime in the history of the Irish State. He also becomes the first to be included in a Witness Protection Programme in the Republic of Ireland. He is guarded 24 hours a day, moved into a different cell every night, has no contact with fellow prisoners and a special chef cooks his food. During Court appearances he wears a bullet-proof jacket and is surrounded by a phalanx of heavily armed police. It is reputed that there is a £3 million price-tag on his head.

I talk to the head of security of a multi-national Irish company who makes it his business to know what is going on in the criminal and paramilitary shadowlands. After an hour he says that he trusts me and will provide another link in this story which is as yet unknown. We talk of the greed and avarice that possess the like of the Warehouseman. The man points out a simple truth – the

Warehouseman could have retired two years ago with £20 million in the bank without the slightest fear of investigation. But like Gotti, got far too big for his boots.

At a later meeting in the Berkeley Court he outlines two other incidents of The Warehouseman's psychopathic appetite for brutality. Gilligan found out that a supplier for his equestrian centre had overcharged him by £1,000, so on the pretence that he was making a further order, he asked the man to call on him. When he arrived at the substantial residence he was given a beating by the gang leader which resulted in a broken arm and leg. Gilligan said he would be back in half an hour and if the man was still there he would break the other arm and leg. The man had to drive away in desperate agony.

On another occasion Gilligan wanted to buy six acres of land from a neighbouring farmer who said he wasn't interested in selling. He received a visit from Gilligan who punched and beat him to the ground. The enraged Gilligan then urinated on the prone body of the farmer.

My security source then outlined in detail the trapping of two members of the Warehouseman's murder squad in Amsterdam on October 10th, 1997. I was given a first-hand account by a senior policeman involved in the operation in which Judas was pinned to the ground by a Dutch Swat team and got such a fright that the coward shat himself.

The Tosser (Brian Meehan), the man suspected of driving the motorbike, defecated in his trousers also and shook like a leaf for hours after he was brought to the station. There's the hard men for you – their bowels are no different than the rest of us – an assault-rifle in the temple knocked the swagger and waste products out of them. Meehan was then brought to a high security prison to await extradition proceedings for murder, drugs and firearms offences. Judas begged to be allowed on the witness protection programme but he is considered a totally unreliable witness and was released.

Each member of this vicious gang is a suitable case for treatment although it would take a strong stomached and minded psychiatrist to take on their case histories. Take Brian Meehan the first lieutenant and head of the drug distribution network. After a career of petty crime started when he was 16, he graduated to bank robbery and served a sentence of 6 years during which he became acquainted with at least one member of the gang. A committed young criminal, he earned the nickname the Tosser because he masturbated in front of a female prison officer while he was detained in the Bridewell police station. The mind of someone who would do such a base thing might be hard to fathom but the action clearly defined his status – scum.

The wheels of the film business move in mysterious ways. Frances McDormand is not available at the time we want to shoot the movie. The American Executive Producer Peter Newman discusses the next move with *Irish Screen* Producer Nigel Warren Green. Nigel was in New York when he picked up a magazine on a newstand. He opened it and there was an extraordinary photograph of a woman who resembled you. Nigel rang me and asked if I had heard of Joan Allen. She's the one, he said, and I agreed. Joan received two Academy Award Nominations for parts in *The Crucible* and Oliver Stone's film on Nixon in which she played Pat. The fact she comes from a theatrical background carries a considerable appeal. But Peter Newman wants a shot at Jodie Foster. We agree with the codicil that she makes her mind up over a short space of time and the fact that she is a Hollywood "A" List Actress in no way affects the integrity of the script and the project which should remain an independent Irish, UK/US Production. After a week Foster's agent asks for an extension which is granted. But all agree that this will be the last. We don't want Hollywood studio baggage. Besides we all agree that Joan Allen would provide perfectly credible casting.

Myself and Nigel travel to London to try to persuade a legendary BBC drama figure, Michael Wearing, to come on board as a Co-Producer. He has already read the script and loves it and has ideas for improvement. Over a long boozy dinner in the Groucho Club Michael agrees to come on board and will put time aside in November to work on the script with us in Ireland. We are delighted with the outcome, in sporting parlance it is a result.

The following morning I audition a Belfast actress, Linda Steadman, who reads for the main part. She is very natural, does not look unlike you but during the session when the medium of the actress seemed to disappear, I was listening to Veronica Guerin and as we absorbed the film version of the acceptance speech at the New York Awards ceremony, I could hear you loud and clear. At the end of the speech we were all close to tears. We all agree that whoever fills the main role will be the very best actress and the one that was meant to represent your spirit in celluloid.

Time moves on, it is now near the end of October but back at home Dublin is bathed in the translucent colours of Indian Summer and we are not quite mourning the passing of Summer. The brilliant hue of the fast-dying light casts its blessed shadow over the golden brown trees in the park, shedding their leafy coat over the grassy edges of the pond where amazingly the fish still jump as if fooled by the season's mellow spirit.

Northbrook Road is carpeted with brown leaves but the trees still host a magnificent russet-coloured shawl. The beauty of this road never ceases to impress me and it is a comforting thought that in a half a year's time the cherry-blossom will be in full bloom. This simple miracle of nature mocks the petty ambition and imperfections of man.

I think of the horror that you were exposed to and wonder how this co-exists with the perfection of the trees in Northbrook Road. Well, of course, this is nothing new in the history of man but that does not make me wonder any the less about the purpose and the purposelessness of life.

The casting countdown continues. Jodie Foster cannot read the script for another two weeks. Nigel wants the script sent to Joan Allen. Peter Newman argues from New York that Joan Allen's name will not secure the finance. Nigel disagrees privately to me. I think Peter does not want to miss the opportunity of landing a Hollywood "A" List actor. The script is sent to Joan Allen. Time is moving on. In the meantime another director, Brendan Burke, starts to work with me on the visualisation of the script, breaking each scene down shot by shot and developing an overall visual style to tell the story in the most dramatic and effective way. The truth of the story is suddenly brought into cinematic relief. I don't think Irish cinema will have seen anything like this, I hope it will have the same impact that your work had on journalism and the public. I have stuck truly and closely to your request not to glamorise the criminal underworld and I believe that their characters and actions will be accurately portrayed.

Nigel gave the script to another director, Terry Ryan (Brylcreem Boys). He read it on the plane and suddenly as he finished the last pages he found tears streaming down from his eyes. I sincerely hope that the import of what you did and the great sacrifice you made will have the same effect on a worldwide audience.

Yesterday Brendan and I worked on a scene in which a junkie and police tout is brutally murdered in the toilet of a rave club. For the rhythm of the scene I have for my sins been listening to rave music supplied by my son Marty who is a rave DJ. Believe it or not, you'd laugh at this, I have developed an appreciation of a music that I previously considered for morons and, after all, who am I to close my ageing mind to the youth drug culture? Didn't I grow up in the era of peace and love, even though I discovered very early on that the mind-expanding drugs had the opposite effect – I stuck to the pints. The beat to this rave sound is mesmeric, underlaid with synthesisers, awash with effects and has great dramatic possibilities. It is of course tribal, but the inner-city gang who collect and enforce for the drug baron are just that and the modern tom-tom – the ghetto-blaster, travels everywhere with them.

Next week, the second week in November, producer Michael Wearing is due to come in from London and co-scriptwriter Colm McCann from New York for a week's work to put a final polish to the script which is in pretty good shape – but in this business, the script is never finished until the last day's shooting.

With regard to the script I ask one question. Would Veronica approve of that? If not, I will not stand over it. And I don't think that I am second-guessing. In the short time we got to know each other, you opened your mind and attitude and above all I want to remain loyal to the things you valued and fought for, and of course, to your spirit, which has never died.

I come across your picture, not one I have seen before and I am overcome with a dull ache of sadness. How I would rather not be curator of your memory but rather look forward to meeting you in Café Java and watch your intense expression dissolve with a smile and listen to your laughter echo among the tables.

A song crosses my mindwaves – one of many I used to play during the early days of putting the script together, after you had gone, and for some reason it now has a resonance. It is on a collection *Best of New Order:*

> *"Everytime I see you falling*
> *I get down on my knees and pray*
> *I'm waiting for that final moment*
> *You'll say the words that I can't say."*

It's the thing of music catching a past atmosphere like the smell of new-mown hay transporting you back to a sacred moment of childhood.

I busy myself, apart from the visualisation, with preparing a file for the lawyers pointing out the proportion of the story which is based on fact. There are two concerns mainly in the criminal arena. Defamation and possible prejudice in the upcoming trials. The fact that we have fictionalised the names does not offer complete protection against legal redress. Depending on the time of the trials and the outcome there would be a scenario in which the film could be distributed everywhere in the world except Ireland. We would all consider this a travesty, but a Senior Counsel, Eoin McCullough is being consulted on the matter. My feeling is that by the time the film is released, the trials would be concluded. The only problem then would be if for some reason or other some of the gang were acquitted. However, I would rather that the film be shown elsewhere rather than the truth of it diluted for the sake of the rights of scumbags who had no regard for the most basic right of all: life.

The script conference gets underway with Nigel, myself, Brendan, Colm and Michael around one table. I am apprehensive about polishing the script by committee. Writers brought into the process, however late, can be surprisingly territorial. I am now in a director's mode and my primary concern is that whatever the fictional licence, the story retains integrity, what Detective Gerry O'Carroll described as the ring of truth. But the presence of Michael Wearing proves to be both sobering and inspirational. He has a brilliant eye for dramatic structure and the logical progression of storyline. The work is incredibly intense. So we play hard at night but this affects neither the quality of work or restraint of temperament. Most surprising of all we all part friends, with only one incident of impasse and possible grief which was resolved. The project involves our heart and soul and I think that the special nature of the project produces a sense of purpose that supplants the normal feeling of ego. The inclusion of Wearing on the production is a big morale booster; his reputation in the arena of hard-hitting drama is legendary, confirmed when we were in a restaurant one evening, when a local producer practically genuflected and kissed his hand.

The script is, according to the experts, in a healthy state, but no one is under any illusions that more changes will be effected. Meanwhile reality seeps in.

The man the police suspect pulled the trigger, Eugene Holland (the Wig), appears in the Special Criminal Court on Tuesday November 18, 1997 on drug-trafficking charges. My contact tells me that he is one paragraph short of charging him with the murder. He intends to complete that paragraph irrespective of the outcome of this trial. Patrick Eugene "Dutchy" Holland is a reputed hit man who is in fact an old man closing on 60 with the physical appearance of a battle scarred rat who has just emerged from a sewer. He is bald with whisps of hair on either side and a beard much in need of fertiliser. His nose has been flattened across his face by some accident collision and his eyes are squinty and mean. He is known as a loner, a sort of modern day western gun for hire who according to police sources relishes carrying out contract work. He is dressed in a cream jacket, jeans and looks as relaxed as if he was in a holiday camp. He holds a notebook and pen but makes sporadic entries, when a particular piece of evidence catches his attention. Occasionally he makes a remark to the prison guards on either side of him. Their response is generally cool. I watch this non-drinking, non-smoking, regular Mass-goer with wonderment. Anger does not enter my thoughts; it is dulled by the grey, clinical atmosphere of the Court. It is hard to believe that this pathetic figure of a man, who at the end of one day's proceedings waves and smiles his thanks to a defence solicitor, is suspected of gunning down at least four people in cold blood and given his Catholic faith would take refuge in the confessional. What fucked-up Freudian theory could possibly explain this behaviour? He certainly does not have the appearance of a man who loses sleep. What makes him tick? If he had a gun shoved into his mouth would he need a nappy?

In common with the detective, I find no room now for hatred in my heart for this murderer. But what is life in prison? No big suffering. Hang him? Too quick. Play a non-stop day and night tape of the agonies of his victims? Too Kafkaesque. I want to lean over the Court railing and ask him what his greatest terror would be. Then I would be tempted to prod him with a needle containing a poison effecting an agonising death to which there is no known antidote. My anger gone? Like a croaking raven, my throat bellows for revenge.

It is strange to contemplate the twelve empty seats where the jury normally deliberate. But no jury would be safe from threat, inducement or intimidation from the core of the Warehouseman's gang. The same way no jury in New York state would convict John Gotti until their anonymity was protected by the court and it remains to be seen how this Special Criminal Court will treat evidence from convicted criminals against others unconvicted for these particular crimes. Despite the intensiveness and thoroughness of the police investigations into the Warehouseman's gang – there are no guarantees under our adversarial system.

The opposing counsels in this case provide formidable talents in criminal law. Brendan Grogan for the defence is theatrical – his glasses remind one of those worn and handled to underscore points by Rumpole of the Bailey. His adversary, Peter Charleton, is boyish, looking somewhat like the school swot but is equally telling in cross-examination by the use of understatement.

Today Thursday November 27, 1997 the three judges will decide the outcome of the defence submission on the constitutionality of the Wig's (Gene Holland's) arrest in Lucan last April. The re-arrest for drug trafficking is not at issue.

It is late November and the weather has turned sour, the grey skies unload an unrelenting downpour. The grip of winter tightens, squeezing the light out of the day. The weeping clouds induce a melancholy, evident in the dirty colour of the pond in the park and the great oak, head down, stripped of its magnificent verdant coat, epitomising the misery of the season.

Down Northbrook Road, the brown leaves have melted into a blood-like mush on the rain-sodden ground while the once proud bearers of their bloom stand bereft, wraiths without the energy to keen for the loss of the life that cheered through the spring and summer. But there is light coming from other sources.

In the first big test of the investigating team, the first of the gang, Eugene Holland, the alleged triggerman, is facing the full rigor of the law but, as we all know, in court there are no guarantees.

From the first day I focus my attention on this so-called ruthless killer. I cannot keep my eyes away from him.

During the opening days of the trial, Holland, wearing the same jeans and cream casual jacket throughout, appeared relaxed and unphased by the slowly unfolding drama. In the words of prosecuting counsel Eamon Leahy when later cross-examining the accused: a man who presented himself as "a spectator rather than a participant".

Occasionally he would lean forward in his seat, appearing to take interest in the proceedings. At other times he would engage the prison officers to his left and right in idle chat of which they clearly expressed less than polite attention. Intermittently he took out a notepad from his jacket and scribbled briefly. While Garda witnesses gave preliminary evidence of arrest, first as part of the investigation of Veronica Guerin's murder and later in the matter of drug-trafficking, Holland cast his eyes around the well of the courtroom like a member of the audience attending a bad play.

To his right, just feet away, sat Jimmy Guerin, your brother. The prisoner made no eye-contact, not one whit of recognition. As the opening gambits of defence and prosecution were enacted, his gaze idled as statement after statement passed him by. One time he aroused himself and for a brief time took some notes which he tore from his pad and passed to his defence solicitor. Perhaps he was seduced by the defence assertion that the simultaneous arrest of his solicitor, Jim Orange on April 9, would prove a breach of his constitutional rights.

For whatever reason, Dutchy Holland's attitude was obscenely cocky. Recognising an old Garda adversary, he raised the two fingers in a jocose manner – hail fellow well met. What did he think he was participating in – an outing to Butlin's? At the end of the second day, he waved and smiled at his solicitor as he was being led away by his prison officers. For the criminal and the gambler it is not over till the fat lady sings and this man believed a remark he made to a senior Garda officer while being remanded at an earlier hearing in Kilmainham Court: "It is not over yet."

To the uninitiated onlooker it seemed that this alleged merciless executioner thought he had the State, the Gardaí and the Special Criminal Court on a hiding to nothing. But the smirk was to be soon wiped from his ugly face as he watched the tide of justice turn against him and reduce the so-called hard man to a twitching, shivering mouse.

It was the appearance of Charlie Bowden, the first man to give evidence under the new Witness Protection Programme, on the morning of the fifth day that took the wind out of Holland's sails and for the first time concentrated his mind on the prospect that at fifty-eight years of age he could spend the rest of his days in prison.

Bowden's evidence against Holland, also known as "the Wig" was delivered with the same coolness and articulate delivery that was shown by Mafia hitman Sammy "the Bull" Gravano when he gave evidence that convicted New York boss, "the Teflon Don" John Gotti, a few years ago. The accused turned his evil eye on his former associate but Bowden never missed a beat. From the moment that the state witness revealed the fact that it was he who prepared the gun and overheard the conspirators discuss the shooting of Veronica Guerin, Holland was a much-changed man.

This was a second blow against his arrogance. Earlier that morning the Court had ruled that he was in lawful detention at Lucan Garda Station after his arrest at Dun Laoghaire on April 9, 1997.

By Wednesday, the sixth day, the prisoner's body language reflected the state of his anxiety. Both his legs hopped nervously off the floor and he continually fingered his flattened nose and sparse beard.

He constantly hunched forward, sitting back occasionally. Throughout the previous days there had been numerous references to his nickname, "the Wig", which appeared on a shopping-list made up by one of the other thugs in the gang. The moniker emanated from his time in Portlaoise where he wore a wig and to the great amusement of fellow prisoners held on to it for dear life while playing soccer matches in the prison yard. Such idiosyncrasy in a fictional character would be considered OTCT (over the crowned top) but for a real person who enacted this scenario, squirm-inducing.

And even Holland did wince a little, but there was further humiliation to come when minus the topper he was called to the witness stand on Wednesday afternoon. The nervousness which afflicted him in the dock turned close to panic when he went into the body of the Court. He gripped the wooden sides of the stand, knuckles bared white, his stumpy ungainly body rigid like a passenger in a doomed plane.

When he was asked a simple question his hands flailed uncontrollably and his voice shook to a whisper. Several times he was asked from the bench to speak louder. Even with the microphone nearer, the pitch of his delivery was close to a squeak, a pathetic contrast to the slick and credible delivery of Charlie Bowden. With an accent uglier and rougher than the blasted heath of his face he stumbled through a series of ludicrous claims.

He claimed that the Gardaí brought him to the interview room at Lucan and some asked questions which others answered. Now that was a new trick which none of us had ever heard before. But, according to the accused, before the Gardaí had begun interviewing each other they collectively recited a *Hail Mary*. That upset him. Deeply, he said. The gallery should have erupted with laughter but this piece of work that is called a man does not inspire comedy. Is it possible that such a perpetrator of evil would actually feign feeling?

He followed this with a tissue of transparent lies about his reason for returning to Ireland in April and the explanation for concealing high-tech transmitting equipment on his person, the purpose of which was to securely transmit a recording of his interrogation to a room near the station where someone would monitor the questioning process on receiving equipment. If there had been any threats, promises or inducements made by the interrogators, Holland could produce a recording in evidence which, if any of those things had occurred, would have certainly led to the collapse of the trial and possibly compromised the murder investigation. This failed action illustrated the cunning lengths that the gang were prepared to go to to either evade or subvert prosecution.

We returned to the wig. It was possible, Holland conceded, that people called him "the Wig" behind his back. But no one said anything to his face. I looked down into the dock at this crumpled excuse for humanity whose face would make a gargoyle assume the aspect of a Botticelli Angel. What misguided vanity made him imagine that a wig would make him any less repulsive?

He wore a wig for years, he explained, for some reason directing his remarks to the bench. It looked alright, he assured the judges.

Perhaps in his twisted logic looking for some sympathy,

Veronica with husband Graham and son Cathal

Photo: Dara MacDonaill, Sunday Independent

Veronica in conversation with her main criminal
contact John Traynor

Photo: Brian Farrell, Sunday Independent

John Gilligan

Photo: Sunday Independent

Brian Meehan

Paul Ward

Eugene 'Dutchy' Holland

*Photo: Colin Keegan
Collins Agency*

Police placing protective covering over the car at the scene of the crime on the Naas dual carriageway

Photo: Pat Langan, Irish Times

Headquarters of the murder investigation at Lucan Garda Station. Top members of the team in conference. Left to right: DG Bob O'Reilly, DS Maurice Heffernan, DG Michael Gaynor, DG Bernard Masterson, DG Michael Murray, Assistant Commissioner Tony Hickey

Photo: Brian Farrell, Sunday Independent

Sniper on the roof. A member of the Emergency Response Unit cuts a dramatic figure on the roof of Green Street Court during the Paul Ward trial   *Photo: Chris Doyle, Irish Independent*

The Irish People express their grief – flowers inside
Independent House in Dublin's city centre

Newspaper stand on
the day of the funeral

*Photos: Kenneth O'Halloran,
Sunday Independent*

Veronica's son Cathal holding Rosary Beads at her funeral
Photo: Kenneth O'Halloran, Sunday Independent

Leading actress Joan Allen on the set of "When the Sky Falls" with first assistant director Robert Quinn

Photo: Martin Nolan, Irish Independent

he informed them that he got it from a man who supplied wigs for people suffering from cancer. There was a plastic suction-device underneath. Thus in a matter of sentences Holland hung himself. For all his cunning and criminal instinct for self preservation he allowed his moments at centre stage to overwhelm any sense of the implications of his evidence. He claimed not to be known as "the Wig" and yet provided a perfect explanation for the nickname which fitted the man who ordered and distributed a huge amount of cannabis from the Greenmount Industrial Estate premises. Eamon Leahy, who with Peter Charleton had throughout been thoroughly undramatic but extremely telling in his line of questioning, did not blink. He asked him about his relationship with Charlie Bowden, the chief prosecution witness.

Holland's answers beggared belief. He had met Bowden on three occasions. The first two to discuss printing flyers for Bowden's hairdressing business. High-class flyers to be aimed at country girls alighting from provincial buses at Busárus. He had earlier put forward an alibi for the day of the murder, stating that he had collected his dole and gone to Bray to collect relations from Peter Mark's. This of course amounted to no alibi because there was nobody to affirm where he was at the vital time. Everyone in the court knew exactly where he was on that day. He knew where he was, but Dutchy in spite of his religious inclinations was prepared to lie under oath. The third time he met Bowden in London "to find out what was going on back home". What "The Wig" omitted to tell the court was that in the course of seeking the state of play in the auld sod he threatened to blow out the brains of Bowden and all that belonged to him if he talked to anyone.

Nice social chat.

He then went on to inform the court that the Gardaí who arrested and interviewed him were all liars, interviewing each other, all relaxed and talking, paying no attention to him. He made no admissions, saw no statements, no notes, signed no statements or notes. Holland made it sound like a pleasant tea party. The Gardaí were there for the craic and in the prosecution counsel's words he was "a spectator rather than a participant".

I know, he said in conclusion, that I am not going to be believed, but that is what happened. His parting shot was classic: "Why didn't they tape me? This would have never happened."

Friday, November 28 arrives and the prosecution and defence teams waste no time in summing up in the morning and the judges waste even less in the afternoon, about six minutes. During the opening lines of the judgement Holland sits between the prison guards for the second-last time. The lights from the ceiling reflect on the shiny bald pate barely concealing the track-marks of numerous failed hair-transplants. The judges have not believed a word that emanated from his mouth: on the balance of evidence presented to them they conclude that Patrick Eugene Holland is guilty as charged.

Reporters look up at Holland for a sign of something. He does not smirk, he seems impassive. The writers will take their own interpretation but, having watched him for the duration, I know he is simply hiding his reaction. The graph of his arrogance has reached its lowest point. The sentence of twenty years is delivered. The prisoner slumps forward. A reporter taunts him and he says, "It's just a job." Another lie. At his age he is unlikely to see the light of a free day and he can lie to himself for the rest of his prison days. For Eugene Holland there will be no Portlaoise Redemption.

There were great celebrations after the last day of the trial among the investigating team and the press corps, not so much out of a sense of victory but a feeling of intense relief. One down, three to go. But there is nothing achieved in this country without the usual dose of begrudgery. I am invited on a discussion about the verdict on Radio Ireland. Eamon McCann is on from Derry. He is a good guy, I like him, but I didn't agree with his analysis. He felt, without knowledge of the situation, that Holland did not get a fair trial and the sentence was in effect for two crimes, murder and drug-trafficking. I pointed out the fact that he was shifting 35-40 kilos of cannabis a week, enough to enable him to offer £1.8 million for a property in Wicklow last year. He had also spent two terms in Portlaoise of seven years each for serious crimes, two counts of armed robbery and possession of explosives, detonators and detonating cord. But still the "liberal bleeding hearts" march onto the parade ground. The excuse usually is to protect the liberty of the "ordinary citizen" but in doing so they begin to excuse the actions of psychopaths and lunatic murderers. Another pundit joins the "liberal bleeding heart" team bleating on behalf of Holland. The judges, he says with fawning respect, got it wrong. Poor Holland is too old to be given an outrageous sentence. Young enough to murder and distribute drugs but too frail to be locked up. Of course he did not attend the trial; he is relying on hearsay and newspaper reports, which he ought to know only summarise the main points of the proceedings.

I won't elaborate but just to take a small point: we all knew that Holland's solicitor was arrested at the same time as his client by members of the Criminal Assets Bureau and was later released. This was the subject of a failed attempt by an eminent criminal lawyer, Brendan Grogan SC, acting for the defence to prove a breach of his client's constitutional right to have a solicitor.

The pundit quotes The People - v - Healy 1990 Supreme Court ruling that there is a constitutional right to a solicitor. If he was in court he would have realised that this was not the issue. The argument was on the basis that the prisoner had a right to a solicitor of his choice.

One way or another the man who a police witness at the beginning of the trial said is the assassin is locked up in the high security jail in Portlaoise and despite later having his sentence reduced to 12 years on appeal will be a pensioner by the time his is due for release. He will have plenty of time to examine his conscience, that is if he has one which I doubt. But unless Catholicism is anything other than a posture then he may be at liberty to consider the prospect of eternal damnation.

On the film-front word has come back from Joan Allen and her agent – they both love the script and it looks like myself, Nigel and Michael Wearing will be going to New York next week to meet with her and her agent. Here is an actress of tremendous accomplishment and maturity; I am, after all this time, looking forward to swapping ideas with the person who can make this incredible woman come to life on the screen. I have had this superstitious habit for the past year of keeping three small-denomination coins in a side pocket of my jeans and a cent piece and an Irish 5p in the back pocket. Mad, isn't it? Recently, for some strange reason the back pocket coins disappeared. The day that Joan Allen received the script, the coins appeared on my dressing-table. There could be an easy explanation, but I didn't look for it. I took this as a sign, as an omen, that at last we have found the right woman to play the spirit of Veronica Guerin. It is not all settled yet but I am sure that you would approve.

I phone casting director John Hubbard and he is delighted with the response and recommends I go to *Face Off* in which she co-stars with John Travolta and Nicholas Cage. Meanwhile Winona Ryder's performance in *Alien Resurrection* is getting a hard time from American critics – "Why is she," they ask, "wasting her talents in an action movie in which her performance is lacklustre?"

John Hubbard says that she will be sorry that she got out of this project. I don't look at it that way – fate has a part to play in everything as it did with us. Ironically I feel that both Winona and Joan have got to get the part that will reveal their full potential, even though there is an age difference of about thirteen years. Joan, with two academy nominations for supporting roles in *The Crucible* and *Nixon*, has been a bit of a bridesmaid and both in *Face Off* and *Ice Storm* she is again in the supporting slot.

Winona should have got a nomination for her performance in *The Crucible* but somehow missed out. I think, and John Hubbard agrees, the time is right for Joan and this is the right part. I have an instinct, without any real knowledge, that this casting is right and was meant to be. Thank God that this time I am going to New York, I don't think I could take Los Angeles at this time of year. John Hubbard and Ros may be there at the same time, meeting David Mamet to discuss casting for his latest film *The Winshow Boy*. He is one of my heroes and I would love to interview him for the *Sunday Independent*. I will try through our American Producer Peter Newman to set up an interview with Harvey Keitel who is starring in Peter's latest production *Lulu on the Bridge*, written and directed by Paul Auster who wrote *Smoke* – a great little film.

I hear Holland's voice on the *Pat Kenny Show* in an interview that took place in London before the rat returned home in April. He came across as the blatant incompetent liar he did in court. He claimed he didn't know Veronica Guerin, only heard like everyone else that she had been shot. He didn't mix with other members of the gang because he doesn't drink or smoke. He used guns in robberies but has never been convicted of using a gun on any person.

But *surprise, surprise!* He has no alibi for the time of day that he allegedly shot you. A criminologist is on the show and he is very disturbed that Holland was given twenty years for possession of £100,000 worth of cannabis and that he should be convicted on the evidence of a supergrass and a confession to police and of all places, in the Special Criminal Court. Another "expert" who did not attend the court case and conveniently avoids the fact that high-ranking members of the Mafia in the US and Italy could only be successfully tried and convicted with the help of their own grasses and witness protection programmes.

No, some lily-livered liberals would like to see these highly dangerous criminals tried by a jury of their peers, conveniently ignoring the fact that those jurors would be threatened and intimidated, and their families burnt out of their homes or shot. Ah but no, the evil scum should be given an easy ride in court and no one should accept the integrity of the judges or the word of a policeman in the process! It is this fuzzy thinking that allowed the rise to unbelievable power of the Untouchables in Dublin and necessitated your fight to expose the true extent of their activities.

In December I travel to New York with other players from *Irish Screen*, Nigel Warren-Green and Kevin Menton; other business for them, my main purpose being to meet Joan Allen at her request before she finally commits. It is almost 10 years since I have walked in the shadow of the skyscrapers of Manhattan and it has not lost its appeal. I still cannot resist looking upwards to marvel at the architectural and engineering feats.

It is close to Christmas and the streets are teeming with shoppers. Amazingly, while the weather is quite cold, the sky is deep blue and the sidewalks are bathed in the stunning orange hue of the winter sun. You had walked these very streets years ago when you came here to receive your award from the International Organisation for the Protection of Journalists – the only western journalist and the only woman. It is such a stark contrast here to the village atmosphere of Dublin but the throbbing pace of life is exciting.

We arrive on Saturday and I am due to meet up with Joan on Monday – time to relax and recover from jet lag.

The weekend flies by and on Monday as we get into the cab to travel to the offices of *Redeemable*, the American Producers, I am overcome with apprehension. At last we have this magnificent actress, the right age and the right look, really interested. Supposing I don't perform well? We all are taking huge risks with this project, but Joan is taking one also by hopefully placing her trust in a first-time feature-film director, after working with Oliver Stone, Nicholas Hytner and most recently Ang Lee in the brilliant ensemble piece *Ice Storm* with Sigourney Weaver and Kevin Kline. *Buena Vista* screened the film in the censor, Seamus Smith's office before we left Dublin and we were all to a man knocked out by Joan's performance as the long-suffering wife of the character, played by Kline, who is having an affair with a neighbour's wife, played by Sigourney Weaver.

The film is a *tour de force* but in exalted company Joan Allen's understated and beautifully subtle performance remains in the mind long after the primary creative colours of the film have faded into the background of memory.

So this makes me a little nervous as well as the fact that the meeting will take place in the presence of Peter Newman, Michael Wearing and the *Irish Screen* contingent. But within minutes of our introduction my fears are allayed. Joan Allen is natural, relaxed and has a smile that echoes yours, the sort that lights up a room and more importantly a screen.

She is given much comfort and security by the fact that I knew you and we had worked together on the genesis of the project. Equally I am comforted by the knowledge that at last we have found the genuine and right actress to translate your spirit.

148

The following morning Joan and I meet in a coffee shop near her home. I have arranged for her to get a whole package of newspaper and television material relating to the story, which she will absorb over the coming weeks while the finance is hopefully tied up.

On that end and on the creative side, both Joan and I agree that there is no room for prima donnas or glory-seekers or fortune-hunters. None of those things have any place around the monument to your memory. Yeah, I hear it – *go and shite*. Not yet, not just yet, Veronica.

I talk to Joan about your humour, your smile and, at times, affectionate nature. All those things, I know Joan can not only embrace but translate, with skill, soul and above all integrity.

We part with a heartfelt embrace. The end of one chapter and the beginning of another in the book of all our lives.

Almost two months later, at the beginning of February, I am back in New York to work on the script with Joan. She has absorbed a large amount of research material in the interim and the first few days we trawl through the mechanics of how the law operates in this country and the complex web that spreads over the different worlds of journalism, police force, the legal system and the figures and territory of crime. It is the same process that you and I went through except this time I am taking your place so that Joan can do the same on the screen.

She is a highly intelligent actress and a sensitive woman. I played her the Lorena McKennitt song "Full Circle" which I hope to use at the end of the film. Joan burst into tears as the enormity of what you did and greatness of your sacrifice was underlined by the heartrending piece of music. We work in the morning at Joan's apartment which she shares with her husband Peter, an actor playing in the musical *Ragtime* on Broadway, and her four-years-old daughter Sadie. In the afternoons we retire to my modest room in the Howard Johnson hotel in Manhattan. The sessions are intense but very satisfying because, as well as the exploration of the strange world of the script, there is a process of bonding and establishing trust. Again a mirror-image of our relationship in the early stages of development.

After one day I know with utter certainty that here is an actress and a woman who can handle the enormous responsibility of translating your spirit to screen with skill, sensitivity and integrity. I begin to experience some joy in the working relationship that we had, safe in the knowledge that you would approve of Joan on every level, as an artist and a tremendous human being. We cover a large amount over the week and I suggest that if Joan has the opportunity to come to Dublin I will get her to read with a number of selected actors so that we can see if particular actors establish a natural chemistry with the lead actress. She is thrilled at this prospect because, in the normal course of events, she would meet the cast on the first day of shooting.

New York is like a giant beehive, humming and buzzing. You wake up to the distant throb of the traffic and immediately the adrenalin begins to pump through the veins. I find a local Irish bar around the corner from the hotel which is frequented by a group of actors working at the Irish Arts Centre, Jim Sheridan's *alma mater*, it is amazing how quickly you can feel at home in a foreign city once the wandering Irish get together.

Joan's latest film *The Ice Storm* has just been released to rave notices and her name and face are all over the cinema magazines. There is one photograph in *Empire* magazine that bears a haunting resemblance to you. It provides further confirmation that this actress, who graduated from the famous Steppenwolf Theatre Company in Chicago, is indeed the best and only choice. Joan accompanies the producers Nigel Warren Green and Kevin Menton to a meeting with head of Sony Classics, Michael Barker, who greets her with a warm hug and the compliment that in his opinion she is America's best actress.

Whether that is studio bullshit-speak or not it is hard to tell but he is subsequently mesmerised by Joan's impassioned plea on behalf of the project. With her status in the theatre and film world, this is an extraordinary gesture but understandable because of the impact that your life and death have had on her. She is not interested in doing any other part or film and wants to come to Ireland as soon as possible. We continue to work on the script. And a story I relate to Joan affects her deeply and by her suggestion will be incorporated into the opening sequence. It was when you were around nine or ten playing soccer on the green with the boys. Anyone who has played football on the square green area in a housing estate knows that at one time or another in the struggle for dominance or the rush to score, a player will thump the ball into high space. All will then watch with horror as the ball either hurtles into a window or crushes Mr Smith's prize roses. There was not much money about so the confiscation of a leather football was a major disaster.

The next decision was which kid was brazen enough to retrieve the ball and risk a twisted ear and/or a kick in the arse. Well, according to a member of your group, it was always a freckled cheeky-faced Veronica who bounded over the gate, retrieved the ball with a disarming smile and ran back to the green. And there was no guarantee, knowing the Mr Smiths around where I grew up, that being a girl would have made any difference.

Three weeks later, at the end of February 1998, Joan travelled first to London to receive an award for Best Actress for her part in *The Crucible* at a glittering reception and she then came to Dublin for four days. The plan was to acclimatise to the surroundings of Dublin and spend a couple of days reading the script with a selection of Irish actors. Despite her experience working with the top Hollywood actors and directors, Joan was very excited at this prospect because a proper period of rehearsal is practically unknown in the movie industry due to financial constraints and/or the availability of actors, many who literally move from one film to the next without a break.

The weather was mild and sunny, so the first day was spent walking around the centre of the city and I realised how much like a tiny village Dublin is when compared to New York. This was a blessing for Joan, because in a very short time she managed to cover quite a lot. The second day accompanied by Detective Inspector Gerry O'Carroll we viewed many of the major locations of the film, travelling by minibus. One of those was the Bridewell Police Station, over the door of which, written in stone, is Juvenal's Dictum – *Fiat Iustitia Ruat Coelum* – which translates: *Let Justice be Done Though the Sky Falls.*

Since we did not want to appear like a troop marching through the august portals, Gerry brought Joan in on her own. They reappeared about fifteen minutes later and as Joan got onto the minibus I noticed that she was pale-faced and tears had stained her cheeks. Gerry explained to me that he had brought her into the cells where two drug addicts had been incarcerated. He introduced her as the matron and the two young men instantly began to beg for heroin substitutes. They were clearly in withdrawal and desperate, and it was also possible that they were suffering from Aids.

Joan described them as looking as if they were close to death. "It brought home to me everything that Veronica was working for and having seen it at first-hand I was overcome with emotion. Here in front of me was the very scenario which Veronica had written and spoken about so many times," she said. Perhaps in a perverse way, this was an epiphany, a solid reminder of the seriousness of the project we were working on and the added responsibility.

The rest of the day we visited the inner-city housing projects that were once totally devastated by the scourge of drugs and we finished off our journey in Ryan's pub in Queen Street where Joan was introduced to some genuine Dublin characters.

The final two days were spent at video-taped reading sessions with a host of actors chosen by casting agent John Hubbard. It was an exciting process because, for the first time, we heard life breathed into the lines of the script. Joan was highly impressed with the depth of Irish talent and over breakfast on the day of her departure to New York we selected the best readings and marked certain actors against the appropriate characters.

Over the next month we had many discussions which for Joan were now more informed by a sense of place and the direct knowledge of the town that she was to adopt for her own.

As for the actors and other people associated with the project who had the privilege of meeting this extraordinary women, John Hubbard summed up their feelings: "I have never experienced such generosity in a top-class actress or such an electric atmosphere in readings."

Very early in this book I made reference to a disgraceful article which by innuendo suggested that you had played a part in the organisation of the first shooting in January 1995. The entry read, "And in the future some pathetic people masquerading as journalists would betray your memory and trust when you were in no position to reply." The deconstruction of Veronica Guerin had begun and it would be continued by spineless writers who were silent while you were alive.

Criticism of the editorial personnel of the *Sunday Independent* was entirely to be expected, particularly in the vexed matter of whether they should have allowed their star reporter to risk her life in the pursuit of stories about the criminal gangs, some of whom had been involved in the first shooting and subsequent beating when you doorstepped alleged drugs godfather, John Gilligan. To question the motives of a newspaper group involved in a circulation war is fair game but as time went on some journalists turned on your personality and motives.

A lot of Irish newspapers are now riddled with so-called thinkpieces, written by "opinion shapers", most of whom have never seen the inside of a school of journalism, not to mention a newsroom and most of whom are incapable of covering a breaking news story or a District Court case. The old journalistic adage reserved for the gutter press "Don't spoil a good story by checking the facts" is increasingly applicable to the practice of Dublin journalism in particular. A lot of the commentators have never heard of the concept of consulting independent sources and simply view the world from the ivory tower of their computer.

You were an old-style reporter with a network of contacts in both the police and criminal camps, a facility for door-stepping and driving the length and breadth of the country to confirm a fact, a work method that exposed the sheer laziness of most Irish journalists. So, your activities not only aroused suspicion but worse still rivalry amongst your journalistic contemporaries. Emily O'Reilly's book *Veronica Guerin – Life and Death of a Crime Reporter, (published April '98)*, typifies this attitude of suspicion and in many instances blatant bias is employed instead of balanced analysis. She discusses at length the ludicrous rumour put about by a combination of jealous journalists and disgruntled criminals that you stage-managed the first shooting in January 1995 to give yourself a higher public profile.

A police contact unequivocally told O'Reilly not to use this rumour as it had been totally discredited. However, the author gives undue prominence to this so-called "thesis". In the matter of your character motivation and desire to continue crime-reporting despite such incidents as the shooting, there were numerous articles in which you gave a first-hand account of the shooting and discussed in a very articulate and logical manner the reasons you intended to continue your work as a crime reporter. And yet none of this material is anywhere reproduced in the book. In death Veronica Guerin was not given her voice.

In the matter of the risks you took, there's more than ample TV, radio and newsprint material in which the subject discusses work methods and journalistic philosophy. At no time while you were alive did any journalist question or criticise you or blame the Sunday Independent for encouraging you to confront the crime barons. No. Such was the political and public outrage then that the journalists that are now having a go at you kept their cowardly counsel until you could no longer reply.

I am to this day trying to work out why a body of so-called educated and professional people should be jealous of a dead person. The only explanation I can find is that, then and now, they felt threatened by your existence, exposed by the fire in your belly, the concentration of your mind and the sheer volume of your work. Among the ordinary people, you had built up a following in the same way that Con Houlihan, our most famous sports writer, had in another arena. And I remember how much he was resented by his fellow writers when he first came on the scene because he was different. He approached his task with a combination of inspiration and enormous energy – he should have been admired by his peers but instead they resented his intrusion on their hitherto cosy formulaic patch. But Con has lasted long enough to be eulogised by those people when he passes across the river into the trees. You have not, and the resentment has not had time to burn out in the breasts of your critics.

Their laziness and shallowness is still brought into relief and always will be. But their petty-mindedness and inability to recognise a true journalistic great will never cease to amaze or dismay me. It just sadly confirms the begrudging nature of the Irish character which permeates all classes and most of all the one that should by nature and practice know better.

It was against such an unsavoury minority background the clock turned towards the second anniversary of the death of the bravest woman ever born in Ireland.

On Easter Sunday April 12, 1998 our son Cian was born in Holles St Hospital. After Ger had been a few hours in labour I left the hospital to go home for breakfast. As I walked through Baggot Street I could see your picture plastered all over the front of the newspapers. It was the inevitable and predictable backlash to Emily O'Reilly's book. Of course it was great to see you being publicly defended but some of the reaction was almost hysterical, thus by default giving some credence to the book.

In the aftermath of Cian's birth I decided to withdraw as director of the film. As well as wanting to spend time with the child, I could forsee difficulties in having the finance completed with me at the helm. The film was the completion of the process we had started and subsequently a monument to your memory – nothing should stand in the way of the film being made, including me. Although I was under no pressure to take this course of action I was mindful of the fact that a modest Irish production company had spent £200,000 on the development of the project. This risk translated to massive loyalty to you, I had to display a similar commitment. Nigel had tears in his eyes when I told him. But I said that I knew in my heart it was the right thing for you and all of us.

Meanwhile the rest of the gang will exhaust every legal avenue to avoid facing the music. Paul Ward is a case in point. It will take two years from his arrest in October 1996 for his trial to proceed. A year after his arrest the Supreme Court rejected an attempt to halt the trial due to start on January 13th, 1998. The trial was adjourned because of new evidence.

In January 1998 the trial opened at The Special Criminal Court. Ward pleaded not guilty to the murder of Veronica Guerin and to the disposal of the murder weapon and the motorbike. The prosecution contends that while Ward was not one of the actual killers, he acted as part of a "common design" to kill or seriously injure Veronica Guerin.

On the following day the judges ruled that Ward's defence lawyers will be entitled to limited access to 40 confidential statements given to the Gardaí. The trial was adjourned when the State appealed the Special Criminal Court's decision.

The High Court refused to permit the Director of Public Prosecutions to seek judicial review of the Special Criminal Court's decision.

On January 23, 1998 The Supreme Court overturned The High Court's decision and granted the Director of Public Prosecution the right to challenge The High Court's decision. The trial of Ward was further adjourned.

On March 4, in The High Court the Director of Public

Prosecution issued proceedings against the Special Criminal Court's decision to allow Ward's lawyers access to the witness statements.

Nine days later The High Court ruled that Ward's trial should proceed in the Special Criminal Court, rejecting Ward's appeal to be tried outside the non-jury court and Mr. Justice Carney also overturned the decision by the Special Criminal Court allowing defence lawyers access to the confidential statements. The prosecution had indicated it would abandon the case rather than disclose the statements, claiming that the disclosure could place the lives of those who made the statements at risk.

This was a highly significant judgment with important implications for the ability of the police to fight organised crime. The judge said that what was involved was a potential conflict between the rights of the people to have organised crime effectively combated by the Gardaí, the rights of those providing information to the Gardaí about organised crime to be protected and the right of Mr. Ward to a fair trial.

"Those who engaged in such crime require a wall of silence to surround their activities and believe that its maintenance is necessary for their protection," he said. "They have at their disposal the resources including money and firearms to maintain this wall of silence and will resort to any means including murder in the furtherance of this objective."

Justice Carney went on to say that "in dealing with such crime the Gardaí had to collect information in confidence from those willing to provide such information knowing that they could face a death sentence if this co-operation became known."

Should such confidence be breached, the Assistant Police Commissioner, Tony Hickey, had testified, it would become virtually impossible to investigate serious crime.

Dealing with the Director of Public Prosecution's application to quash the Special Criminal Court Order (for limited access of confidential information to the defence), the judge said that it was, in his experience, unique that such an order should be sought during a trial.

In most cases any question of judicial review should be dealt with after the trial. But such an approach in the present case would have led the Director of Public Prosecution to abort the trial and the people would have been deprived of their right to have "a particularly heinous crime prosecuted to a verdict of either conviction or acquittal."

It was his view that the Special Criminal Court had, in deciding to disclose the documents to Mr. Ward's lawyers, exceeded its jurisdiction in fundamentally altering the established relationship between defence lawyers and their client. It was no answer that Mr. Ward had consented to his legal team having sight of the statements on the terms that they were not to be disclosed to him without leave of the court.

Mr. Justice Carney said that the Special Criminal Court would examine the forty statements and determine whether any of them might help the defence case, help to disparage the prosecution case or give a lead to other evidence. On the basis of that examination, the court would determine which, if any, of the statements should be disclosed to the defence.

In conducting its examination of the documents, the

court would be exposed to material prejudicial to Mr. Ward. But Justice Carney accepted the court's assurance that it would nevertheless be able to deal with the case fairly. He did not consider it necessary that the Ward case be dealt with by the ordinary courts.

There was one last act in this long-drawn-out legal saga when, at the end of July 1998, The Supreme Court ruled that Ward would go on trial before The Special Criminal Court and upheld The High Court decision that his lawyers would only be allowed access to the statements once The High Court had examined them and decided which, if any, of the statements should be disclosed to the defence.

Brian Meehan has appealed the Amsterdam District Court ruling of October 1997, that the extradition application by Gardaí is valid under Dutch law. His appeal failed on June 9th, 1998 when the Supreme Court rejected the arguments of the defence and declared that Meehan's extradition should go ahead. The defence then used the last avenue of appeal to the President of the District Court in the Hague. On September 3rd the ten-month legal battle ended when the appeal was again thrown out. An Air Corps plane then returned Meehan to Ireland and he was brought to the Special Criminal Court and charged on eighteen counts, including murder, possession of firearms and ammunition and possession of cannabis and importation of cannabis into the State. Meehan was a sorry sight compared to the cocky criminal who waved to relatives during his first Dutch court appearance almost a year before. He has aged visibly and the *Sunday World* greeted his return to face justice with a screaming headline – *The Evil has Landed*.

From the time of his arrest in October 1996 at Heathrow

Airport by custom officers, where he was caught with £300,000 in drug money, John Gilligan has fought the original charge of possessing the proceeds of drug trafficking and extradition to Ireland on the foot of eighteen warrants to face charges of murder, importing cannabis and possession of firearms over no less than twelve court appearances. Finally on January 12th, 1998 the High Court in London turned down his appeal against extradition but Gilligan's defence applied successfully for a hearing in the House of Lords. This judgement is not expected for some time, but it is considered by legal experts highly unlikely that it will be successful.

In the interim at another hearing in Woolwich Crown Court his lawyers opposed a further remand on having possession of the proceeds of drug-trafficking and Gilligan claims that he is being held in inhuman conditions in Belmarsh Prison which Amnesty International has criticised. He says that he will plead guilty to the charge if he is not extradited to Ireland. The judge expresses some sympathy with his situation but remands him in custody until the end of April.

John Traynor remains at large as is "Fatso" Peter Mitchell and Shay Ward.

Ward was finally brought to trial in the Special Criminal Court on Tuesday, October 6, 1998 before three judges, Mr Justice Robert Barr, Presiding, assisted by Mr Justice Thomas Ballagh and Mr Justice Esmond Smyth. The opposing legal teams comprised the best criminal lawyers in Ireland. On the defence side were Chief Counsel, the legendary Patrick McEntee SC assisted by Barry White SC and briefed by Michael Hanahoe.

While the prosecution was headed by the younger but

no less wise Peter Charleton SC assisted by familiar team-
mate, the tall and imposing figure of Eamon Leahy SC,
assisted by Tom O'Connor.

The first week, just three court days in all, laid the
ground and in evidence the court would hear shocking and
horrific details of the gunning down of the country's
leading crime reporter and also details of the genesis and
operation of a drug gang whose resources and ruthlessness
were designed to match anything the Mafia or Colombian
drug cartels had to offer. By the end of the week, I was
haunted by all the same feelings and emotions that
followed your death in June 1996 and, on the last day,
found my colleagues' faces were blanched by strain,
concentration and shock.

Heretofore all we had to face was the enormity of the
fact of your death. We had been spared the detail, the
cynical, clinical brutality of the execution. I had, of course,
imagined it and the terror of the final moments, but my
imagination was placed into transparent insignificance
when faced with the reality. No conviction could ever wash
away the pain of hearing what those heartless bastards did
to you.

On Tuesday October 6, 1998 Paul Ward sat in the dock
of the Special Criminal Court, casually dressed and wearing
gold-rimmed glasses.

For all intents and purposes he could have been a
minor civil servant in appearance and he remained
impassive through the proceedings; just waving and
passing whispered messages to his family and girlfriend
Vanessa Meehan (sister of co-accused Brian), who
occupied the gallery, at the end of each day before being
returned under escort to Portlaoise prison. The prisoner

and the court and all its attendants were to hear, over the week, evidence of the most dramatic and harrowing nature. This prosecution of Ward and other members of the gang involved in the planning and murder is undoubtedly the most complex and comprehensive in the history of the State.

And it raised issues outside the main thrust of the trial which pertained to the matter of a fair trail for the accused on one hand and the ability of the Gardaí to fight crime in general and protect the confidentiality of their sources of information on the other. This issue had dominated the pre-trial actions in the highest legal arenas in the land and the eminent defence counsel, Patrick McEntee, was not going to let the matter go away. In a trenchant submission on the opening day Tuesday October 6, 1998 he claimed that the defence was entitled to see forty statements by twenty witnesses for the prosecution, which the State had claimed successfully as privileged on the grounds of the danger to those witnesses.

He declared dramatically that without access to those statements the defence was a black hole. There could be, he argued, material in those statements prejudicial to his client Paul Ward – without seeing them he just could not know. There are limits, he declared, to which the most vigilant can exclude prejudicial material – which was a veiled reference to the bench. And he pointed out the very salient fact accepted by both the bench and the prosecution: the trial could stand or fall on the credibility of the main prosecution witness, supergrass Charles Bowden.

Chief Prosecution Counsel Peter Charleton SC replied in his usual understated fashion and said that none of the witnesses who had made the privileged statements were witness to the conspirators of the murder and thus were not relevant to the defence and he went on to say that, while he acknowledged that Bowden's evidence was crucial, in statements by Ward in custody, the State had enough to pursue a successful prosecution. The presiding judge, Mr Justice Barr, with the consent of Mr Justice Ballagh and Mr. Justice Smyth, agreed to read the statements and make a ruling on Thursday, after an adjournment on Wednesday.

Mr Charleton then opened the prosecution case and won his first mini-victory on Thursday morning when the court ruled that the privileged statements "per se the contents of the documents offer no assistance whatsoever to the accused in his defence and are prejudicial to his case. The prosecution claim to privilege was well founded and the documents ought not be disclosed." Mr Justice Barr said that if it emerged the contents of any of the documents had become helpful during the course of evidence, the court would look at them again.

It was then down to the nitty-gritty of the case as Mr Charleton painted a graphic history of the criminal gang who from importing small amounts of cannabis in 1991 became hugely rich and hugely dangerous. Dangerous because with the importation of cannabis and cocaine was an arsenal of arms.

Chief State Witness, Charles Bowden, joined the gang in 1994, but it was not until he returned from holiday in the United States in 1995 that he became aware of who else was in the gang. Among these was Ward and others not to be named by direction of the Court. Bowden, Mr

Charleton said, would give evidence of a discussion in a car at the Strawberry Beds early in June 1996 involving Ward and other members of the gang about the planning of the murder. During the discussion, reference was made to having the reporter followed by a motor vehicle and a motorcycle from Court in Naas and the fact that someone would be watching her. Six bullets were loaded into a .357 magnum revolver and it was readied by Bowden for the shooting.

While Mr Charleton conceded that there was no forensic evidence linking Ward to the murder as the gun was never recovered and the motorbike dismantled, he said alleged verbal admissions while in custody were sufficient to convict him of the crime. There would also be a log of mobile telephone calls between Ward and one of the men on the motorcycle on the day of the murder.

As Mr Charleton began to describe the calibre and character of the arms it became clear to court observers that the gang was amassing resources of destruction of which the king of the Colombian cartels, the late Pablo Escobar, would have been well proud.

It later emerged that this gang had just as much respect for the dead as the living – none.

In a follow-up operation four months after the murder a detective squad was led by Bowden to a Jewish cemetery on the Old Court Road in Tallaght on the outskirts of the south side of Dublin. At the rear of the grave of a woman named Miriam Norcupp a huge cache of sophisticated weapons and ammunition was found.

The account from ballistics expert Detective Sergeant Pat Ennis of the discovery and breakdown of the cache was dramatic enough but the setting produced a hush among the press corps. Not even the most imaginative of writers would produce such a scenario of desecration of a grave and insult to the family and memory of the deceased.

In concert was the evidence of the assassination on the Naas dual carriageway on June 26, 1996. Both the witness police accounts provided a picture of unrelenting ruthlessness and horror. No crime novel can reproduce the awful effect of hearing the last moments on earth of a woman that most of the reporters in court knew, loved and respected. A lorry driver described the arrival of a high-powered motorbike at the top of the queue of cars stopped at the Green Isle Hotel junction of the Naas dual carriageway and the sound of backfires. A man saw the bike speeding around a corner on one wheel; two nurses had attempted to render assistance to the mortally wounded reporter. The faces of the eye witnesses blanched as they recalled a moment they would never forget.

Through the grey veil of the dispassionate evidence, black shadows of the nightmare returned. If I didn't believe that your spirit and soul would triumph and be forever shining beyond the jaws of death, I would have felt like screaming aloud. But nothing, not even the drone of observed fact could obliterate the rage and sadness inside. I have replayed the event of June 26, 1996 a thousand times. You would think that one more time would have made no difference, but it did. And there was worse to come. This person they named as the victim, Veronica Guerin, was you, is you.

Police witnesses from a variety of technical bureaus were called, photographs of the scene of the crime, inside and outside the red Opel Calibra car were exchanged. The trajectory and characteristics of the .357 magnum bullets

167

were discussed. There were, it was claimed, similarities with ammunition found in Miriam Norcupp's grave. The irony of that fact escaped no one – bullets taken from a grave to create another. The technical mantras went on but the sense of horror never diminished.

It reached its climax when on Friday morning October 9, 1998 the State Pathologist gave his evidence. John Harbison is a man who delivers his evidence in a professional and precise tone. There are no high or low notes, just fact. The entry and exit points of the .357 magnum bullets, the shards of glass and debris that punctured the skin, the bloodstained newspapers on the passenger seat, the dark stain on the driver's seat, the mobile-phone cord wrapped around the deceased's left arm. I presume, he said, she had been reaching for her mobile phone.

Later the details of the post mortem in the morgue of the James Connolly Memorial Hospital; further precise notes on the bullets that ripped through the body of a tanned woman with greying blonde hair and bright healthy teeth.

One bullet entered the lower end of the mastoid muscle, and the subclavian artery was severely lacerated. This appeared to be the most serious injury and the principal cause of blood loss. A second bullet, found in the left collar bone, had come from below. There was bleeding in the left lung and he found a half litre of blood in the left chest cavity and a third of a litre of blood in the right chest cavity. There was also laceration of the right lung on the outer surface and a bullet had passed through the lower lobe of the right lung. A bullet had also cut across the liver and this was the bullet that had injured the right lung.

The Court was hushed as Dr Harbison's educated delivery elucidated the physiological destruction. I glanced at some of my colleagues occupying the last two benches. Normally, however much under pressure, they exchanged notes, jokes, smiles. Their faces reflected the import of the evidence, pale, frozen masks of horror.

I looked back and upwards at Ward in the dock. He returned my look with interest – behind his glasses, his eyes narrowed. The subtext read, "What the fuck are you looking at?"

Dr. Harbison continued – he said he had deduced that the first bullet had hit the glass and would have been deformed causing a larger wound than the calibre of the bullet would normally inflict.

The trajectory of the bullets suggested that Ms Guerin was going over to her left but he was unable to say if it was due to her falling or trying to evade her attacker. Two of the bullets entered the back, the lower at the base of the spine. One had passed through the fleshy part of the upper right arm and then entered the breast and travelled across the chest in a slightly downward trajectory.

I had this vision in my mind, fighting a nauseous sensation in my stomach, of a slow-motion action replay and I could see the same thing in the eyes of the experienced court and crime reporters. Shards of breaking glass and debris puncturing skin, blood spraying against the windscreen and over the newspapers on the passenger seat, the headlines melting into the sodden newsprint, the gun barrel exploding once and then again, again, again, again and again. Reaching for the mobile, the life energy of the profession, the last line, careering crazily away. And all the time, an eternity of time, beyond the scientific measure of a great pathologist, in which you were gripped by unrelenting and unending terror. I cried silently – my heart pounded with anger. Dr Harbison concluded his evidence.

The cause of death was shock and haemorrhage caused by multiple bullet wounds, causing lacerations to both lungs and the artery supplying blood to the right arm.

There is a merciful silence. The air is full of restrained sighs, a mixture of collective anguish and gratitude that it was over. The press corps had covered many a case in which post mortem evidence was an integral part.

But for once they knew the victim. This could never be just another case.

The afternoon returned to the more mundane evidence – that of the arrest of Paul Ward. Inspector Padraig Kennedy told the court that he arrested the accused in Windmill Park in Crumlin on October 16, 1996 under Section 10 of the Offences Against The State Act on suspicion that he had information relating to the possession of firearms on the Naas Road on June 26, 1996. The decision to arrest Ward had been taken on October 9 after Charles Bowden made a statement on October 6 implicating Mr Ward in the murder. Ward was taken to the interview room at Lucan Garda Station, but questioning had been postponed when the prisoner stuffed paper up both his nostrils, causing slight bleeding from the nose. The detective made no effort to seize the bloodstained tissue because he believed Mr Ward was a drug addict at the time.

Inspector Kennedy said he believed Mr Ward had met the two men who were on the motorcycle on the day of the killing and had helped dispose of the murder weapon.

In the second week the court heard evidence from Doctor Lionel Williams who visited Ward on October 16th in Lucan Garda Station where he had been detained. Ward requested physeptone, a heroin substitute, and while the Doctor formed the opinion that he did not need it, he left 40 mls in a steel container in the public office to be administered on request. The prisoner alleged that he did not receive the medication until the following day.

Over the period of his 48-hour detention he was questioned by a team of twelve of the police force's most experienced interrogators and he claimed that one, Sergeant Cornelius Condon, had assaulted him. He pointed out a red mark on his neck to Dr Williams on a subsequent visit on October 18th. Over the period of his detention the prosecution claimed that the accused had made several verbal admissions, which he did not sign, implicating himself in the disposal of the gun and the motorcycle used in the murder.

These alleged admissions were made after visits from his mother, Elizabeth, father, Michael and girlfriend, Vanessa Meehan who were in simultaneous custody. The visits, according to the defence, were unsolicited. Ward was released from custody at 3.30pm on October 18th but was immediately re-arrested outside the gates of Lucan Garda Station and detained under Section 25, The Misuse of Drugs Act 1997.

This whole period of custody would come under close examination by the defence team and form the platform for five submissions to be made during what is known as the *voir dire* or trial within the trial, challenging the admissibility of Ward's verbal admissions and the lawfulness of his detention in Lucan. Another issue was a previous arrest on the night of October 8th at the Green Isle Hotel.

After security staff at the hotel had observed Ward and some companions acting suspiciously in the car-park and later, after he had booked into the hotel (under a false name) in the corridors, police were called and Detective Garda Sheeran arrested Ward at gunpoint in his bedroom. He was brought to Ronanstown station where he was detained on suspicion of being involved in a robbery at the SDS Depot on the Naas Rd. Detective Garda Sheeran then left the station to meet an informant who told him that he had got the wrong "'Hippo' Ward." Apparently several of his family go under the same nickname.

On his return to the station Detective Garda Sheeran ordered the prisoner to be released. The defence contended that the reason for this arrest had been fabricated and that in fact Ward had been arrested on the same charge for which he had been detained in Lucan eight days later. If this was true the arrest and detention at Lucan would have been invalidated. This formed the substance of the defence submissions which began the trial within the trial during the second week. If even two of these submissions were upheld by the court, the prosecution case would collapse and Ward could walk away a free man.

The leading defence Counsel, the legendary Patrick McEntee, had affected the demeanor of a wounded hawk when his submission in relation to the confidential statements was refused during the first week's proceedings but he was back to his old self when he tore

172

into a long list of Garda witnesses accusing them of laziness, incompetence and lying. Dealing with the Green Isle Hotel arrest, when the accused was taken out of bed at gunpoint, he boomed, "you pointed a gun at a sleeping man?" "I wasn't taking any chances" replied Detective Garda Sheeran. "With a sleeping man?" asked the counsel in an incredulous tone. "They aren't always sleeping" replied the Detective to laughter in the court.

Continuing his evidence Sheeran said that he had left the station after his arrest to meet his informant and learnt that he had arrested the wrong "'Hippo' Ward." The prisoner was then released from custody at 2.45am. Wasn't it extraordinarily stupid, suggested Mr McEntee not to ask which "Hippo" the informant was talking about in advance of the meeting? If the Ronanstown arrest and detention was dodgy in any way the Defence Counsel could not seem to make any headway against the arresting Detective, who clearly had a lot of experience in court proceedings.

Then Mr McEntee turned his attention to Dr Williams who gave chapter and verse on his encounters with the prisoner on two occasions during the detention. He was not amenable to suggestion or interpretation. He said he could find no evidence of withdrawal symptoms nor any sign of needlemarks on the prisoner's arms and added that Ward seemed physically well and fit for interview. On his second visit he did notice a red mark on the prisoner's neck but received no request to examine him. Ward had asked the doctor not to tell his mother that he was on drugs. Garda Catherine Moore said that she had given Ward the 40 mls of physeptone left by Dr Williams on October 16th, at 9.10pm.

A succession of Garda witnesses was then called to give evidence to rebut suggestions that a Detective visited Ward in the middle of the night. There was also evidence that Ward's girlfriend Vanessa Meehan who was in custody in Ballyfermot station was brought to visit Ward in an interview room at Lucan between 10.25pm and 10.35pm on October 17th. After the visit she was detained overnight in Lucan Station.

The second week of the trial concluded on Friday October 16th, 1998, two years to the day since the accused had been arrested.

The trial within the trial continued on Monday October 19th, 1998, when security staff at the Green Isle Hotel gave evidence of the circumstances surrounding the accused's arrest in the early hours of October 8th, 1996. If there were any doubts about the validity of the arrest in terms of motivation the staff's evidence would be vital to prove that the genesis of the arrest was genuine and not sparked off by a tip-off that Ward was on the premises. The defence insisted that all hotel personnel directly involved be brought to court to give evidence but the net result was to provide strong corroboration to the police accounts of the incident. Uncharacteristically Mr McEntee succeeded in shooting himself in the foot. The evidence of security men Noel O'Neill and James Downs in particular established without doubt that Ward and others had been acting suspiciously and the fact that the address given in the register did not check out confirmed those suspicions.

The security staff had been vigilant because a robbery had recently occurred at a hotel in Leixlip orchestrated by people who had booked into rooms under false names.

Detective Garda Sheeran and his team responded to the security staff's request to come to the hotel and subsequently arrested Ward. Even if the defence team were to lose this battle there were still four other major grounds to pursue, the first of which related to the lawfulness of the Lucan detention.

On the morning of Tuesday October 20th,1998 the accused's seventy-four year old mother, Elizabeth, was called to the witness box by the defence. Having been helped to the box by one of her daughters she then gave details of her detention on the same day as her son's. On October 18th, 1996 she was brought from Cabra Station to Lucan. "I seen Paul," she said, "and I was crying, are you alright? What happened to you Paul? What happened to your neck? Who done that to you? Was it the same man who beat you up years ago? He said it was Cornelia' (sic). Ward was referring to Detective Cornelius Condon.

Up in the gallery the large Ward family contingent held onto every word their mother uttered. The accused's stoney-faced impassivity had been softened. It was clear that Elizabeth Ward was in every sense of the word a matriarchal figure who inspired both fear and love in her son. He had pleaded with interrogating officers and with Dr Lionel Williams not to tell his mother he was on drugs. Such confused morality is typical of the Dublin criminal class. He had been arrested on suspicion of having knowledge and part in a brutal murder and yet his greatest worry was that his ma would find out that he was taking heroin. Then again it could have been just one act of a play written by the prisoner to convince the audience that he was unfit to be interviewed.

One way or another the Mammy was playing a

blinder in the box for her errant son. She described being driven at high speed from Cabra to Lucan and said she had been petrified with fright. She dissolved into tears while recounting an alleged insult from one of the police officers. She said that the Detective told her that, "all my sons were bank robbers and all my daughters were whores. I said all my daughters are married and have families." Mrs Ward then wiped tears from her eyes.

In the dock Paul Ward abandoned his straight-backed posture and leaned forward. Behind his gold-rimmed glasses tears welled up in his cold eyes. Mr McEntee had the witness, Mrs Ward, in the box for over an hour, mainly chronicling her own alleged mistreatment at the hands of the police so Mr Justice Barr presiding interjected and said that 99% of her evidence was irrelevant to the issue of alleged physical mistreatment of the prisoner while in custody. The issue he added, was whether she had seen evidence of mistreatment and earlier on Mrs Ward confirmed that she had seen a red mark on her son's neck.

Mrs Ward left the witness box with the aid of her daughter and while passing the dock extended her hand to the accused who grasped it tightly. His girlfriend Vanessa Meehan was not called to the witness box but the defence maintained that her visit, along with Mrs Ward's, was part of a scheme to induce a statement of admission from him. The defence submitted that the accused made two statements following the visits of Ms Meehan and his mother. While it was suggested that he had made a request to see his mother he had made no request to see Ms Meehan and if these visits were used to "overbear" his will, in an attempt to make him talk this would have constituted a breach of his constitutional right to silence.

The prisoner was next to be called to the witness box. Acknowledged as a former thug in his own neighborhood and later by his own admission part of a dangerous and ruthless drug gang, his demeanor gave no hint to his background or activities. Nonchalantly placing his right hand over the box he had the appearance of a minor bank clerk on an embezzlement charge. If the gravity of his situation impinged on his mind, there was no art to find it in his face or his relaxed manner. He chose a moss-green poloneck sweater and olive-coloured jeans for his appearance. His strong Dublin accent was affected with a respectful tone finishing each sentence with "me lords".

Ward told his counsel Barry White SC that he had gone to the Green Isle Hotel on October 7th 1996, with one of his brothers and that they were driven there by another brother. He was concerned with allegations that his brother was a drug courier. He booked them into a hotel room and his brother left. He was "sound asleep" when he was struck in the face. He saw a plainclothes policeman and a uniformed guard with a gun.

He was told he was being arrested for firearms on the Naas Rd in June 1996 and handcuffed and taken to Ronanstown Station. He said that on October 16th, 1996 he was arrested outside his house and told he was being arrested under Section 30 of The Offences Against The State Act for firearms on the Naas Rd on June 26th 1996. He was taken to Lucan Station and later told a doctor that he was a drug addict and needed physeptone. He said he did not get any physeptone until he was given it by Dr Lionel Williams on October 18th. He went on to claim that on that morning he was assaulted by a Detective

Cornelius Condon who, "all of a sudden gave me a smack across the left side of my face. I jumped up. My hands were in my pockets and I got into a struggle with Mr Condon and the other Detective," he said. He claimed he ended up bent over the table with Detective Condon holding his neck in an armlock. Later his mother noted a red mark on his neck. But despite the alleged assault and deprivation of medication Ward proudly claimed that he never broke his silence to the team of interrogating officers. "The reason is, it would have been showing weakness." He claimed that he did not ask for his physeptone, "because I had the feeling that had I asked for pity, I would have been refused."

While Ward was a calm witness he displayed a very poor understanding of the implications of his statements. The whole defence point of the deprivation of medicine was that it meant that the prisoner was unfit for interview. And he would have been much more vulnerable and likely to break his silence. And yet Ward had just blithely announced that he showed absolutely no weakness in his resolve not to answer any questions.

Prosecution Counsel Peter Charleton SC was quick to pounce on this contradiction. So having been assaulted and deprived of his medication for a long period did he feel he was unfit to be interviewed? Did he agree perhaps with the doctor who felt he had been fit? "I'm not an expert," was the accused's weak reply. Mr. Charleton suggested his story was "complete and utter nonsense" and that much of his evidence was "a fantasy." Ward adopted an indignant tone and replied "that's not true my lords, that did happen."

After finishing his evidence Ward returned to the

dock looking towards his family in the upper gallery as he traversed the court. When he reached the dock he removed his gold-rimmed glasses and polished them. His performance as a witness was not a patch on that of his mother, forty years his senior. The prosecution cross-examination was to the point but not particularly rigorous and most surprisingly did not explore an alternative explanation for the red mark on his neck, such as the possibility that it was self-inflicted.

The trial within the trial had concluded and on the following day Wednesday October 21st both defence and prosecution teams made submissions on the issues raised. Patrick McEntee SC told the court that if the visits of his mother and girlfriend were used to overbear Mr Ward's will in an attempt to make him talk when he would have otherwise stayed silent, then his constitutional right to silence had been breached. The court was told that after Vanessa Meehan's visit to Lucan on October 16th, Ward had made a verbal admission. He was visited for sixteen minutes by his mother on October 18th and made another verbal admission. The legality of his arrest and detention in Lucan were also challenged, Mr. McEntee arguing that his constitutional rights were further breached by non-compliance with custody regulations – he was deprived of his medication and was assaulted during interrogation. The defence also claimed that his earlier arrest and detention in Ronanstown Station was for the same charge and thus invalidated his subsequent arrest on October 16th.

Replying to the defence submissions Peter Charleton SC said the court had the benefit of hearing the state of mind of the accused when he gave evidence and not once did he say he was upset by the visits or that they had any impact upon him.

Mr Justice Barr said the prosecution must establish that the arrest and detention were at all times lawful and that the prisoner was given the benefit of the doubt of lawful procedures. Referring to the visits he said, "the prosecution must establish that there was a good, valid, acceptable reason for bringing those two ladies to see their nearest and dearest." The court would not give its judgement on the issues before 2pm on the following day, Thursday. As it transpired the judges needed more time and did not return until Friday morning October 23rd. On that morning the galleries of the Special Criminal Court were packed to capacity. Tension was etched on the faces of the leading members of the Gardaí team involved in the interrogation of the accused. This was to be expected because, not for the last time in this case, it was in fact the police who were on trial, not the accused Paul Ward.

In the gallery Jimmy Guerin and his wife LouAnne looked tense and nervous while by contrast the Ward family seemed completely at ease. The prisoner was relaxed and chatted to members of his family in the gallery above him. A buzz of conversation moved around the benches below, there was the sound of shuffling of papers and the heavy footsteps of the court guardians. All sound ceased. The air of tension mounted as the three judges entered at 11.42am. After they had sat down there was nobody who could have read the minds of Justice Robert Barr, Justice Esmond Smyth or Justice Thomas Ballagh.

Then Mr Justice Barr placed the printed judgement in

front of him and began to read its contents out. For the next forty minutes, in measured and clear tones, the judge outlined the issues, the opposite arguments and the court's conclusions.

Dealing with the Green Isle arrest Mr Justice Barr said, "the accused's explanation for his presence in the hotel was that he had been concerned about the safety of his brother Séamus who was on the run from the police and he had arranged with the latter that he would conceal him for the night by taking a room under a false name in the Green Isle Hotel. He could not explain why his brother wandered about the premises leaving fire doors open nor did he know at the time why Séamus had left the hotel or even that he had left the bedroom.

He alleges that he had no knowledge that Séamus had any intention of leaving the bedroom that night. He further alleged that he learnt subsequently that the reason why his brother Séamus left was to see his wife. If that were true it defeated the alleged purpose of going to the hotel and taking a room there and it exposed Séamus Ward to the risk of arrest by police which it was alleged he was anxious to avoid. The court rejects the accused's explanation for his presence at the hotel and the account he gave of his arrest there. The court is satisfied beyond reasonable doubt that Detective Garda Sheeran arrested the accused under Section 30 of the 1939 Act on foot of his *bona fide* belief at the time of arrest that the latter had been involved in the SDS robbery on October 2nd. The reason why the accused was released is not relevant to that determination.

The second ground – the alleged unlawfulness of his arrest by Inspector Kennedy on October 16th, depends upon establishing the accused's contention as to his arrest by Detective Garda Sheeran and therefore in the light of the court finding in that regard does not arise."

Two of the defence submissions had been thrown out but there were three left to be judged upon – nothing was certain yet.

Mr Justice Barr moved on to the third submission – the alleged failure to accord the accused his basic right to appropriate medication for purported substantial heroin withdrawal symptoms and to take proper steps to satisfy themselves that he was fit for interrogation at all material times.

Mr Justice Barr made reference to the two visits by Dr Lionel Williams and his conclusions regarding the physical well-being of the prisoner and the fact the accused had never complained to anyone about withdrawal symptoms. "In the light of foregoing evidence the court is satisfied that the accused was fit for interrogation at all material times and that he was not deprived of his right to necessary medicine or medical attention."

The court clock crept towards ten minutes past midday and just above the clock in the dock Paul Ward showed no sign of emotion or any indication that the tide had begun to turn against the defence. Mr Justice Barr then dealt with the fourth submission, the alleged assault by Detective Sergeant Condon and he concluded, "the court rejects the accused's account of the alleged assault and is satisfied beyond reasonable doubt that no such event took place." In football parlance the score was four nil. But the fifth round, if upheld, could prove to be a Pyrrhic victory for the prosecution because this provided the other main pillar of evidence along with that of former gang-member-turned-state-witness Charles Bowden. Mr Justice Barr pointed out that this submission had arisen during the trial within the trial and did not form part of the defence's original submissions on the lawfulness of the accused's arrest and detention. This related to the visits which the defence claimed was a form of oppression brought to bear to weaken the prisoner's resolve and breach his right to silence. No explanation had been given by the prosecution as to how, why and for what purpose the visits were arranged. He went on to say that it would be fundamentally wrong and a denial of justice to allow the prosecution any advantage which could have emanated from such wrongdoing on the part of the police. The issue was only raised and fully presented in the closing address of the defence counsel. Vanessa Meehan had not been called to give evidence and the purpose of Mrs Ward's cross-examination had been to demonstrate that her detention was unfair and that she had seen a red mark on her son's neck.

The accused in evidence never said anything about pressure being put on him by the visits. He was silent about what transpired between him and the women. "Finally the defence team had been aware of these meetings and if any improper behaviour had emerged on the part of the police then it would have been ventilated in the evidence and cross-examination of the Garda officers." Mr Justice Barr concluded his judgement as the court clock neared twenty-three minutes past midday. "In the light of the aforegoing assessment is there a reasonable possibility that the visits of Ms Meehan and

Mrs Ward to the accused were orchestrated by the police as a stratagem to oppress the accused and cause him to take a course of action favourable to the prosecution case against him? That is the essence of the issue. The court is satisfied beyond reasonable doubt that no such possibility exists. Accordingly that ground has also not been established. The court is satisfied beyond reasonable doubt about the legality of the accused's arrest by Inspector Kennedy on October 16th 1996 and his subsequent detention and interrogation at Lucan Garda Station."

I flashed over to Bewleys in Mary Street the previous day where my colleague *Sunday Independent* crime reporter Liz Allen and Jimmy Guerin had coffee and discussed the prospect of the Judgment from the perspective of pure speculation. Jimmy was quite pessimistic and Liz cautious. I felt that it would go in favour of the prosecution, with the worst-case scenario of the verbal admissions being discerned inadmissable but not preventing the trial proceeding.

Jimmy passed me in the body of the court with a broad smile on his face. "Five nil," I said without any sense of exultation because there was a long way to go and we were all conscious that Patrick McEntee would use all his considerable experience and skill to destroy the credibility of the main prosecution witness Charles Bowden and, while the verbal admissions had been allowed, experienced court reporters were well aware that they were on shaky ground because the alleged police orchestration of family visits to Ward as a submission was only an afterthought on the part of the defence. With time to examine the issue more thoroughly, to bring Vanessa Meehan to the stand, and cross examine the officers in depth, then the picture could change. As Ward was led away for the lunch recess after the judgment he waved and chatted to his family in the gallery.

When the trial resumed for the 4th week the following Tuesday, October 27, Mr McEntee lost no time in dealing with the issue and showed no effect of the defeat of just a few days previously. First he dealt with Charles Bowden. It was inconceivable, he said, that there would not be discussions by the authorities with Charles Bowden about his future and he wanted to know what undertakings had been given to the chief prosecution witness, what he had waived and what was conceded. There must be a record of the negotiations. He wanted access for the defence to any memos between the Gardaí and the Department of Justice. The process then began of cross examination of the police interrogators who had handled Ward in Lucan.

The next day the defence were allowed access by the court to the two files referring to Charles Bowden. Edward Comyn SC for the Attorney General agreed to the access with one *caveat* – the phone and mobile numbers of the police on the witness protection programme should not be disclosed.

The shadow of Bowden was then thrown over the court. Again and again the name of the man who by his own admission provided and cleaned the gun used in the murder added tension to the cross examination of police officers who had interrogated him at Lucan station. Bowden, who is serving a six year sentence in Arbour Hill for drug trafficking, was arrested on October 5, 1996 and investigating officers gave evidence that it was after they had statements made by Bowden that they arrested and interrogated Paul Ward. Bowden had led a division of the police team to a Jewish cemetery on the outskirts of the city at Old Court Road in Tallaght. In the early hours of the morning under the cover of darkness the team removed the stone slab over the grave of Miriam Norcupp and found a number of guns and ammunition similar to those used as the murder weapon, which the accused is charged with disposing of as well as the motorbike.

These details raised expectations that the state prosecution witness would be called to the box before the end of the week and it was that he would have a more horrific tale to tell than that which he had recounted in the Holland trial. Anything to relieve the dull trend of cross-examination which towards the close of the week prompted Mr Justice Robert Barr to interject while defence counsel Barry White was in full flight – "we have heard this *ad nauseum,* please move on". The week could have been entitled *"Waiting For Bowden"* but as Friday's proceedings opened in Green Street Court everyone acknowledged the fact that the state witness was unlikely to take the stand until the following Tuesday. Another witness for the defence, Vanessa Meehan, who signed herself in the court as "girlfriend" of the accused received extensive mention in the proceedings without being called to the box. The defence were to further explore the theory mentioned in the trial within the trial that her visit in particular was orchestrated to pressurise Ward into making a statement.

"She knows nothing, leave her out of here," Ward was alleged to have said to interrogating officers. He told

Detective Sergeant Bernie Hanley that a certain gang member "would go fuckin' crazy if I involved her. She wasn't even in the house that day."

It seemed that earlier when she was imprisoned and questioned she stood by her man answering "I don't know" to every question. The interrogating officer Inspector Kennedy claimed that she had made a request to see Paul Ward and "felt it was not unreasonable and I was going to facilitate her."

Detective Garda Hanley had earlier denied that he had told Ms Meehan that the Gardaí were not interested in her or Mr Ward and that if she asked Ward where the gun was he would let them both go home. It was an old familiar song – your word against mine – which left one with the inevitable conclusion that if the versions of events were so conflicting then one party was lying.

Taking the oath then is almost meaningless when the stakes are so high – the police are under huge pressure to secure a conviction and no one relishes the prospect of a mandatory life sentence, not least Paul Ward. "Liar" was a word much bandied about by the defence as the trial entered the fifth week and high drama.

The presence of metal detectors in the hallway on Monday November 2nd raised expectation about the imminent arrival of the chief prosecution witness but there were still about half a dozen police witness to be examined about the arrest and detention of Mrs Ward and the alleged verbal admissions. Assistant Commissioner Tony Hickey was to be called by the prosecution but Mr McEntee successfully objected saying that his evidence was irrelevant and probably highly prejudicial to his client.

The day passed, all eyes were on Tuesday. The next morning the press gallery and the court was packed to capacity. There were two garda witnesses to be dealt with but already we knew that the chief state prosecution witness had arrived before the court sat and was being protected in the basement of the historic building. Earlier in the morning a motorcade of garda and army vehicles ground to a halt outside the court, a half a dozen heavily armed soldiers spilled onto the street as the motorcade, including a large van with blacked out windows, moved quickly into a side yard, the doors closing quickly behind. Above the ornate portals of the 18th century building a marksman with a visor provided an image reminiscent of Darth Vadar from Star Wars. Back in the court as the last of the police witnesses was giving evidence, I thought about Bowden and the fact that without his participation there would be no trial. And because of the fact that, in common with any member of a large criminal organisation, he turned against his own he will be reviled among the criminal classes and be despised by society as a whole for being involved in the first place.

And as all criminals who turn "state's evidence" he will have to show real grit, restraint and great character in the witness box. The Mafioso lieutenants who broke the code of *omerta* in the United States and Sicily proved despite their vile activities that they had great strength to take the step in the first place and subsequently survive under cross examination. I think of the words of Tomas Buscetta, a Sicilian Mafioso who turned on his own –

"I want to make it clear that I am not a stool pigeon. I am a penitent in that my revelations are not motivated by base calculations of personal interest. I have spent my life as a Mafioso and I have made mistakes for which I am prepared to pay the consequences without asking for sentence reductions or special treatment. In the interest of society, of my children and other young people I intend to reveal all I know about the cancer of the Mafia so that generations can live in a more human and dignified way."

While Bowden would not match such a high standard of redemption – he had a deal which gave him immunity from prosecution for murder – he would have to display nerves of steel and a similar commitment to make his evidence both credible and effective.

And of course he faced one of the country's most skilful and feared cross-examination experts in Patrick McEntee SC whose skill for searching questioning would reduce a Jesuit to tears within minutes. Bowden had come clean about his part in the murder but what would the eminent defence counsel make of his motivation?

At 11.20 am Charles Bowden took the stand. He was bearded, with heavily oiled thick black hair, and wore a smart blue jacket whose bulk was clearly inflated by a bulletproof jacket. For the next two days before his cross examination was adjourned temporarily, this man unfolded a tragic tale of Shakespearian proportion that *"would harrow up thy soul and freeze thy young blood"*. He spoke in quiet tones and quickly established the fact that he would be an articulate and intelligent witness for the state. Only once did he look at Paul Ward when asked to point him out in the court.

From then on he faced sideways and fixed his eyes on the prosecuting and defence counsels. Whether he had been coached to do this or not, it proved very effective as if focusing on his Nemesis would somehow dilute his powers. But first he answered questions from prosecution counsel, Eamon Leahy SC. He told Mr Leahy that he came from a large family in Finglas, a working-class suburb in south Dublin, left school early, joined the army in 1983 and left in 1989. In the army he was a prize-winning marksman and a Black Belt in karate. After leaving the army he worked as a bouncer and having separated from his wife and three children he began to experience financial difficulties.

He was a member of a kick-boxing club in the inner city where he met a drug dealer who took him on to supply Ecstasy to named customers, using his job as a bouncer in the Hogan Stand Pub as a cover. People called to the pub and he distributed about 2,000 Ecstasy tablets a week for which he was paid five hundred pounds. He got out of drug-dealing and went back to school but at the end of 1994 his girlfriend left him and he returned to drug-dealing with the same man, who engaged him this time to distribute cannabis resin in large quantities. Bowden rose through the ranks quickly to become the quarter-master general of a huge drug gang.

He rented lock-up premises in various locations in the city from which the drugs were distributed to a network of dealers. Eventually he rented bigger premises in the Greenmount Industrial Estate in Harold's Cross from which between 250 and 500 kilos of cannabis were being shifted every week. On occasions a shipment of guns would come in with the cannabis and he and other members of the gang stored them in two graves in a

Jewish cemetery on the outskirts of the city. Not only was Bowden a good and trusted lieutenant but his expertise with firearms increased his value to the gang and the gang leader, who at all times kept his distance from direct involvement in the operation. He cleaned and maintained the weapons which presumably would act as a deterrent to rival gangs who might invade their patch.

But the gang leader had other ideas for the use of a 3.57 magnum stored among the cache. During the early part of 1996 he told other members of the gang that he was "pissed off" because he had been charged with assaulting Veronica Guerin. Bowden recalled three conversations that members of the gang had about her. On one occasion four members of the gang were in a car in the Strawberry Beds area when one of them asked him about the whereabouts of the 3.57 magnum. Bowden told him it was with the other weapons in the Jewish cemetery in one of the graves. There were two other conversations at the apartment of the gang's first lieutenant. He recalled that the day before the murder he cleaned the magnum, loaded it with six rounds of ammunition and left it on a table with six spare rounds.

The prosecution witness's account was sparse and to the point and delivered without a trace of emotion while he described the prelude to a monstrous tragedy. Graham was in the gallery as was Jimmy and his wife on the opposite side. You could hear a pin drop in the chamber. I felt the blood begin to drain from my face and Bowden's matter-of-fact voice only served to create images as I thought of the phone call I made to you on Tuesday night June 25th and the sense of unease I felt afterwards. I remember the phone call on the Monday night when we discussed the adjourned hearing of the assault case and the emphasis you placed on the danger to your work practice if you lost your licence after the court hearing in Naas on Wednesday. And I shuddered at the thought of the simultaneous plans that were being hatched while we had this discussion. I recall the fear and loathing of the incident outside Kilcock court. For a moment these memories blotted out Bowden's voice and I felt an immense sense of sadness which laid a heavy weight on my heart. I knew that I was not alone in this feeling and I did not have to wonder about the weight of the hand that laid on Graham's heart and on Jimmy whose reaction to your death seemed to have caused a rift in the family. Grief is not always a unifying emotion.

Gradually Bowden's face and voice came back into focus. He was referring to a week before the fateful day. Each Friday evening the gang of five met in the first lieutenant Brian Meehan's apartment to distribute profits and make plans. The subject of Veronica was brought up by Meehan, the only member of the five to have regular direct dealing with the gang leader. He explained that if the gang leader went down for the assault case then the gang would lose the only contact with the overseas supplier of the drugs and consequently they all had a lot to lose. On this occasion the conversation was about the court case in Naas and there was speculation about whether there would be police protection. But there would be a watch put on the journalist and someone would be detailed to follow her and someone to shoot her.

Eamon Leahy's questioning was directed towards establishing fact and the witness was under no pressure. After lunch that was to change when Bowden faced the wrath of Mr McEntee's cross-examination technique. For forty minutes the counsel tore into him over an incident while he was an army corporal and was court martialed for a vicious assault on a number of young recruits – shades of *Full Metal Jacket*. The perpetrator had said he made a full and frank admission at the time and had been stripped of his rank. Mr McEntee wanted to know why he was subverting the investigation at the time and why was he behaving like a bully boy.

The formidable barrister had but put a shot across Bowden's bows. Bringing the witness back to his early introduction to the drug trade he asked about the criminal contact he met in the kick-boxing club.

"You went to him and said 'I hear you employ drug dealers. Give me a start'."

The insulting sleight of delivery began to put the witness under pressure. He drank his water more regularly, a clear sign of nervousness. But he never averted his eyes from his interrogator. Paddy McEntee is made of stern stuff, he has a razor-sharp mind, a firm grasp of the language of the court and an undetectable cunning that can transform an apparent blind alley into a highway.

But Bowden concentrated and, if anything, his replies became more articulate and so the testimony went on, painting a fascinating and horrifying portrait of the ruthless methods, the corrupt dealings and the degenerate life style of the drug gang. The witness emerged from this tale as a man of indulgences, a goodtime Charlie with a fondness for women which though often requited just as often ended with the woman leaving him. Mr McEntee branded him a greedy gangster with no morals and an "inveterate liar".

Bowden did not disagree and the more familiar he became with the jibes and insults and of course the incontrovertible facts the more assured his responses became. Bowden was hoarding his money in such diverse hiding-places as a laundry basket, which at one stage contained forty thousand pounds. He removed the money as the police dragnet closed in on him. He was panicky and frightened, he said and he planned a shopping trip to London "to get away from it all".

At this stage he was living with his girlfriend Juliet Bacon (whom he later married in prison) in a suburban housing estate called the Paddocks. But it was not his girlfriend who he was bringing on a shopping trip to London to be financed by fifteen thousand pounds kept in a plastic bag.

"Tell us about your lady friend, who wasn't your lady friend" asked Mr McEntee. Bowden claimed to be in love with the woman who is now his wife. Counsel enquired as to why he was bringing the other woman to London. "I wanted to impress her. I wasn't having an affair. There was no question of sexual intercourse." Mr McEntee derided the answer. What was he doing bringing her without the knowledge of the woman he said he loved? Bowden appeared to cave in "infidelity is what it was". One way or another there was no opportunity to go on this fantastic shopping spree for, on the Saturday October 5, 1996, Bowden was arrested before he could leave the house. His drug-dealing days were over. On

Wednesday afternoon the chief prosecution witness left the box for a temporary break while the court dealt with more basic evidence such as the prosecution's supportive account of a record of mobile and landline telephone calls between Paul Ward and the driver of the motor-bike on the fateful day June 26, 1996.

The evidence was circumstantial but did provide a link between the accused and the murder gang.

Nineteen calls were made on June 26, 1996 between Ward and the man who drove the motor bike, Brian Meehan. Four calls were made by the motorbike rider to his land-line at his bungalow. They were at: 08.14 (duration 17 seconds), 08.28 (14 seconds), 08.45 (9 seconds), 23.11 (6 seconds). The same man made six calls on his mobile phone to Ward's mobile phone: 11.02 (24 seconds), 12.49 (3 seconds), 13.06 (37 seconds), 13.32 (29 seconds), 13.52 (44 seconds), 15.23 (16 seconds). Paul Ward made 9 return calls on his mobile at 08.56 (5 seconds), 09.08 (5 seconds), 11.48 (9 seconds), 13.55 (16 seconds),14.34 (19 seconds), 15.48 (20 seconds), 15.51 (20 seconds), 23.11 (25 seconds), 23.12 (4 mins 5 seconds).

On Monday November 9, the twenty-first day of the trial, Charles Bowden returned to the witness box, and he looked fresher and more relaxed for the break. He needed it because for the next three days and the last act but one of the prosecution case he would be subjected to the most stinging verbal battering that any witness in any trial has had to take. In the light of the alleged orchestration of Ward's verbal admissions and the purely supportive nature of the phone records, the outcome could be decided over the next three days. The defence would explore every avenue to discredit the witness and destroy his credibility.

It was approaching the end of the marathon fifth day of cross-examination of the chief witness for the prosecution. He should have been on his knees exhausted, but Charles Bowden, who by his own admission had a bigger part to play in the murder than the accused, Paul Ward, was defiant. He kept his eyes firmly fixed on defence counsel Patrick McEntee and answered in strong and sometimes aggressive tones.

Bowden ridiculed counsel's suggestion that he had met two other members of the gang in Moore Street on the afternoon of the crime for the purpose of disposing of the murder weapon. It was ludicrous, he claimed, to suggest that two members of a gang who were regularly searched by Gardaí for contraband cigarettes would bring a recently-fired gun into a crowded city-centre street, after killing a journalist.

It was as if the mauling he had experienced the previous day had energised him or he sensed a certain tiredness in the questioning which covered the same ground again and again. And of course, some of that ground was vital. For example, the alleged meeting in Moore Street in which Bowden told the court, one of the gang, Brian Meehan, directly involved in the murder that day, referred to the unspeakable act as a "good job".

And Bowden told how the gang spent the night of the murder whooping it up in The Hole In The Wall pub. And it is not to be forgotten that Bowden was among them. But earlier, at the start of the week, there was even more disturbing evidence from the one-time gang member now under 24-hour protection in Arbour Hill Prison. A hush came over the court as Bowden told how he had been finally converted to giving evidence against his former comrades and had decided to stop making lying and contradictory statements to the police, to save his own skin.

What Bowden was about to do was not save his skin but condemn himself and his nearest and dearest to a future in which they would always be looking over their shoulders and a present in which they cannot do any of the ordinary things that make life worth living, without the presence of an armed detective.

Drawing a deep, quivering breath, the one-time goodfella and former goodtime Charlie poured a glass of water with a shaky hand. "I had made admissions that put me and my family in danger and I was entirely aware that I was part of the murder and fully aware of that part. During questioning I had a cover story and was prepared to continue lying and did for a long time. During one interview the detectives produced photographs of Ms Guerin dead in the car.

Before that I had blocked out everything to do with the murder but this brought reality home. Now I could not detach myself from it. When I saw the photographs of the girl lying in the car I went to pieces. I thought that my wife and children were going to suffer but I wanted to tell everything. I was faced with the reality of the horror. My brain superimposed Julie's face and the face of my children on the photograph. To clear my conscience, and I know that sounds trite, I had to tell."

His responses to Mr McEntee varied. Sometimes the response was quiet, sometimes clear irritation came through and other times the raised voice gave his emotion away. At this stage he was close to tears, his voice choked with suppressed emotion. He reiterated his contention that while he had loaded the gun, he did not think the gang leader who organised the hit would be "stupid enough to carry out his threat".

Be that as it may, on the night of the murder he did have a noisy drunken crowd back to his house and played techno rock which Mr McEntee explained fell under the category of "loud and unpleasant, much to the annoyance of his neighbour who was told in no uncertain terms by Mr Bowden where to go when he called in to complain".

Make no mistake, Mr Bowden was a nasty piece of work but his admissions and assertions have a ring of truth.

But would the ring of truth be sufficient to secure a conviction? Was Bowden a self-serving liar who was shopping other members of the gang to save his own skin? Or was his evidence, as Mr McEntee put it "all part of your carefully laid scheme to involve Paul Ward and minimise your own part"?

Mr McEntee had exposed a number of discrepancies in his evidence. In an earlier statement to the police he had put Ward at the party in The Hole In The Wall and then stated later that he was not there. There were also discrepancies in his account of his hairdressing shop which he purchased in Moore Street and which he claimed was a legitimate business to give him a respectable front and a vehicle to explain how he could pay the mortgage on his house in the Paddocks. Despite denying it was a front for drug-dealing, it transpired under cross examination that some transactions had taken place in the salon.

At 12.25 p.m. on Wednesday November 11th after a marathon session in the box, Bowden looked exhausted but he seemed to have withstood each punishing round remarkably well. However he left questions as well as answers and it would be up to the court to properly address those as well as to assess the veracity of the answers. His departure concluded the state's case and the next witness kicked off the defence efforts to clear the accused. And it was Paul Ward who stepped into the same spot previously occupied by Bowden on November 12th. In the trial within the trial he had proved himself a confused and unintelligent witness and so it was a calculated risk to expose his mental limitations to searching cross examination. He would have to balance fact with fiction and on his form that would prove difficult.

How freely would he speak, I wondered. The answer came quickly – very freely. He began by saying that he was a victim of Bowden's lies and he claimed that the prosecution witness poisoned the police with allegations that he was involved in the murder. While I looked at this skinny pale-faced man with a sort of lopsided jaw and twist in his mouth and his stories of being a drug-addict I felt anger rise in me. I don't mind the lies that were going to pour out of his bloodless lips – people like him are born to lie – what really annoyed me was the affectation of innocence. But all the same, I know he is not very clever and is quite capable of hanging himself and others unwittingly.

He described a trip to Saint Lucia with the gang leader and the gang for a wedding in March 1996. The gang were slagging the boss about the assault charge. They were all having great gas. "He was laughing and saying he wasn't going to jail on an assault charge."

"What's so funny about being beaten up?" asked the prosecuting counsel, Peter Charlton S.C.

"No, no, it wasn't that. It was more the fact that your man was so convinced he'd escape the rap," insisted Ward.

Unwittingly he had put his foot in it. And he admitted they had joked about the journalist. Ward was talking off the top of his head blissfully unaware of any trap the prosecution counsel might spring. In truth Mr Charleton would not have to strain himself in that regard.

Ward said he had spent forty thousand pounds to "furbish" (sic) his mother's house. When asked what he did between 1994 and 1996, he replied, "I was selling cannabis, tobacco and cigarettes." He said he had made £300,000 in that period from cannabis. He admitted he had been in the apartment of the first lieutenant Brian Meehan mentioned by Bowden on numerous occasions and said he was a friend of the man. He agreed with Mr Charlton that this man was "a major drug dealer in Dublin". He agreed with Bowden's evidence that the drugs gang paid the gang leader £2000 per kilo and then sold it on for a profit.

Despite this admission he accused Bowden of being the real villain. "That man should be in the dock. I was asked to do what that man did and I refused because I knew nothing of Ms Guerin's murder." The following day, Friday, November 13, Ward admitted that he used to collect money from his clients and to carry the money in plastic bags – up to £20,000. He said that he collected up to £3,000,000 in cash in one year and most of the money was sent to the gang leader. He said he had visited an equestrian centre owned by the man in Co. Meath and taken his daughter there to ride horses.

Ward said he had not seen the gang leader in the aftermath of the killing but had spoken to him on the phone and also admitted that he had spoken to several of the gang members. They had discussed the killing afterwards but all denied having any part in it. He admitted there were 19 calls between his land-line and mobile and another mobile phone but could not remember if the calls had anything to do with drug-dealing or about arranging for his girlfriend's son to go to school. Ward then returned to the dock which he should have in truth never left. He had little time to reflect on his performance as his girlfriend Vanessa Meehan was the next defence witness.

Vanessa was in the box a short spell on the Friday and told Mr McEntee that she had been going out with the accused since she was 17 and moved into the house on Walkinstown Road when she turned 20 in May 1996. Ward was taking heroin and she noted symptoms such as weight loss. She had tried to get him off the drug but he kept going back to it. She resumed her evidence on Monday, November 16. Wearing a white shirt and fawn trousers she cut a glamorous figure in the box and one wondered how she had got involved with the spindly weedy Ward. She said that at the time he looked really washed out and was under nine stone. He would detox for a while and then go back. She said that they didn't go out much but other members of the gang would call to the house. In June of 1996 he was on physeptone. In that month they had gone on a week's holiday to Santa Ponsa with other members of his family. They arrived back in Dublin in the early hours of the morning of June 23. They stayed in that night and watched a video.

On Tuesday the 25th Paul got a phone call from his mother saying that her niece Natasha, who was also a drug-addict, had stolen a clock which had sentimental value. Her boyfriend borrowed her car, which he had bought for her for £10,000, and went looking for Natasha. When he found her on the street he hit her a slap in the face and brought her back to the house. There was a bruise on the left side of her face when she arrived at the house. He told her to get off drugs and that he would help her. She was to stay in the house and detox.

Up to this point Vanessa had been a calm and impressive witness but it became increasingly obvious that what she was leading up to was to provide an alibi for Ward for the following day June 26. So Natasha stayed with them all that day while Ward who had a huge problem, according to his girlfriend, staying off heroin, suddenly put all his time and effort in getting his niece to kick the habit, a magnanimous gesture to say the least just after having hit her a box in the face. From June 25 the bungalow in Walkinstown Road had been transformed into a detox clinic. On June 25th Paul left the house for a short while and returned with a large bottle of physeptone. The following day Paul got up early. She didn't get up until 10pm and Natasha didn't surface until after midday. Paul got her physeptone and Natasha lay on the couch from 1.30pm while Paul sat on a chair watching television. "No one came to the house during that time or later," she declared, "and no one came to the back of the house."

Between 6pm and 9pm she went over to her mother's house to tidy up and during that time she heard of the killing on a news bulletin. It was of no significance to her at the time. "There was a shooting on the Naas Road and a journalist was after being shot," said the lovely unflinching Vanessa. She had heard the journalist's name being mentioned in relation to an assault case while they were on holiday in St Lucia. She heard that the gang leader was involved in a court case at that time and read about it in the paper later. And yet, as stated in her evidence, when she heard of the killing it had no significance. "I thought it was a horrible crime. I may have mentioned it to Paul but to be honest I can't remember."

"To be honest" is a phrase that punctuated many of her answers. A very endearing habit, if it were to be true. She said she had never been in The Hole In The Wall Pub but she had been in The Brasserie in The Hibernian Mall in the company of other members of the gang including Charles Bowden.

After spending a couple of hours or more in her mother's house on the night of June 26 she returned to the bungalow, still being used as a detox clinic. Paul and the patient Natasha were there. She couldn't remember if there was any discussion about the murder. "I can't remember," became another of Vanessa's mantras. Natasha stayed for a week and apparently got better but surprise, surprise her punch-throwing mentor fell by the wayside again. "Paul went back on the heroin in August and ended up in a detox clinic in London for 2 days." She said, "There was a second detox visit to London but it did not work; he went back on the drugs between the middle to end of September."

Around that time two detectives called to the house and left a card for Paul asking him to contact them. "He was shocked because he had nothing got to do with it. He said to me, 'I don't know what they want me for'." Vanessa's memory is excellent for certain detail, particularly the days up to and after the killing and, of course, her own arrest and detention in Ballyfermot Station and the subsequent visit to Ward in Lucan Station where he was detained.

Now if the murder was of no significance and she had lapses of memory she had a very clear picture of her experience at the hands of the police in Ballyfermot. "They were aggressive towards me, screamed that I was lying, they threatened I would be charged as an accessory. I was confused and frightened. If you don't change your statement one detective said, you are going to be done as an accessory. I eventually changed the statement. I was crying a lot. I was terrified."

On October 17, 1996, the detectives told her that she was being brought to see Ward in Lucan. "The detectives said I was to ask him where the gun is. They would let me go if I asked him this. I did not ask to see him. I was more concerned about myself to be honest. I was not too concerned about Paul."

This was an extraordinary statement coming from a woman who had stood by her man through the thick and thin of heroin abuse and who was now in detention in another station on a very serious charge. She didn't want to see him, she was much more concerned about saving her own skin. Vanessa Meehan was brought to Lucan to a different room from Ward. "In the hallway I heard a commotion. I could see into the hallway. They were screaming at him to come into the room. I was crying. I called out to him to come in."

At this stage the witness dissolved into tears, wiped her

eyes and struggled to continue. "I was very upset, I asked him to tell them where the gun was. 'If I asked you they would let me go home.' He said 'I'll be out before you, I'll collect you'." Vanessa's eyes filled up once again and she paused as she mopped the tears away.

She went on to say that even before she was arrested she left and went home to her mother's house because the addiction had got too much for her. He had asked her to go back but she said no. But clearly Vanessa Meehan was hooked. She had been split up with him a week before the arrest, had herself been detained and interrogated over a 48-hour period before being released on October 18. And in the intervening period of time her lover had been in jail for two weeks awaiting trial. It would be more than most young twenty-something women could take. But Vanessa must have been made of metal, steel or sterner stuff.

When asked by defence counsel Mr McEntee whether she was still in love with him she replied "yeah" and dissolved into minor tears for the third time.

Under cross examination by Eamon Leahy SC she admitted that she knew that Ward had not got a legitimate job. He sold cigarettes and tobacco. And she suspected he sold hash. A great deal of money was spent on the refurbishment of the bungalow including the installation of a jacuzzi and he bought her a Lancer car worth £10,000. And yet Vanessa never asked him where the money came from. There were trips to the best boutiques including Brown Thomas and thousands of pounds had been left lying about the bungalow and then deposited in a hiding-place in the attic. In 1996 there were no less than three foreign holidays including 10 days in St Lucia in April.

Vanessa, falling into the habit Paul Ward had in the witness box, confirmed that the gang leader and other members of the drug gang were there and she admitted she knew how they made their money. And previous to the holiday she had met the gang leader about twice. Once in his equestrian centre in Meath and another time in the first lieutenant's apartment. She couldn't remember the exact conversation.

For the observer the selective memory of Vanessa was all the more astounding when put against her graphic and emotional recall of the time in custody and particularly the exact detail of the detective's conversation. But when it came to the drug gang, everything became hazy. She had heard a conversation about the assault of the journalist by the gang leader but "I can't remember the exact conversation." She recalled an article on the same subject but of the contents "I can't remember exactly, I think it was about [named gang leader] assaulting Ms Guerin". Of the conversation in St. Lucia she said, "I wasn't really listening." Mr Leahy asked if there were any other conversations about Veronica Guerin. When asked again, she replied, "I can't really remember." The prosecuting counsel really hit the nail on the head of her evidence. "Why is your memory of June 26, 1996 so clear?" The reply was palpably lacking in conviction. "Because it was the start of Natasha living with us," she said in an uncharacteristically weak tone. Under cross examination, the witness, so poised when questioned by the defence, faltered. She stated that she heard of the killing on a news bulletin between 6pm and 9pm and yet Ward had read it in *The Herald* around 2pm or 3pm. It had slipped her memory that Ward had left the house "for five minutes to go to the Spar. He bought me flowers and ice-pops for Natasha". She then became confused saying that he often bought her flowers and yet she was "so shocked by the flowers I didn't notice the newspaper".

"And was there any mention of the death of Veronica Guerin?" enquired Mr Leahy. "Not that I remember," she replied. As Mr McEntee might have put it, this evidence beggared belief. A murder of tragic and gigantic proportion in Irish terms, matching that of JFK in 1963 and there is no mention of it in the Ward household that afternoon despite the fact that the accused brought back a copy of *The Evening Herald* with a report of the killing under huge banner headlines. It appears that the woman of the house, who was used to getting flowers from her beloved, was so shocked by the commonplace gesture that she paid no attention to the newspaper. She then said she may have mentioned it to him later after coming back from her mother's house. "I don't know whether he said he heard about it. I just mentioned it in passing. I didn't really take notice of it, to be honest, so I can't really remember."

There were other subsequent conversations about the subject and the link with the gang leader but it was all vague and she wasn't paying any attention to the newspapers. "Even when the media interest vastly increased?" asked counsel. "I can't remember exact conversations." For a young woman who loved to dress from the best boutiques, boogie in the best clubs and pubs and splash out on foreign holidays, the sudden insulation from the world around her ill befitted her social habits. This was not a lady to bury her pretty head in the sand.

She had played a blinder in the first half with the defence, with assertive and at times tearful evidence, but in the second half she assumed the mantle of a shrinking violet and her evidence wilted accordingly. If one ever lightly edited her sentences all that would have been left is "I don't remember". Before she left the stand at 4.25pm she conceded that her evidence may have assisted Paul Ward "but it is the truth". Vanessa then returned to join the rest of the Ward family in the upper gallery for the remainder of the trial.

Evidence of Natasha Madden, a defence ballistic expert Jonathan Spencer, an army officer on Bowden's career in the defence forces and Sean Molony, a journalist and neighbour of Bowden's who claimed there was a big party next door on the night of the murder, took up the bulk of the week. The trial was winding down towards conclusion and small loose ends were being tied up before the prosecution and defence teams made their final submissions.

At 11.25am on Thursday November 19, the 29th day of the trial Eamon Leahy SC opened the prosecution's final submission.

"Having played a part in a pre-arranged plan to shoot Ms Guerin and is complicit in a crime and in law guilty of the crime itself. If the court is satisfied the accused participated in a plan to kill or cause serious injury to Ms Guerin, he would be guilty of murder."

Eamon Leahy faced the three judges of the Special Criminal Court and outlined the State's case against 34-year-old Paul Ward, a self-confessed drug dealer, who is charged with the most sensational murder in the history of the State, the murder of former investigative reporter Veronica Guerin. Concise, cool and meticulous in his identification of the reasons why Ward should be found guilty of the murder, Leahy spent just over 95 minutes outlining those precise reasons.

Mr Leahy suggested that the prosecution's case rested on four pillars of evidence, any of which were sufficient to convict Ward on a charge of murder. These pillars were two sets of interviews conducted with two different teams of detectives, the evidence of the supergrass Charles Bowden, and the existence of telephone records showing 19 telephone calls between Mr Ward and another member of the crime gang on the day of the murder.

On the day of the murder, Mr Leahy said, a powerful motorcycle driven by one man and carrying an assassin, drew abreast of Veronica's car. The State is not contending that the accused was present at the Naas Road, or that he was the driver or the pillion passenger. It is, however, contending that he played a part in plans to kill Ms Guerin.

Mr Leahy suggested that the judges should draw inference of guilt from the first telephone contact Ward had with gardaí – the telephone call which Ward made to Sergeant John Gerrighty in the Incident Room at Lucan Garda Station on July 17, 1996 – just 21 days after the murder. Mr Leahy outlined Sergeant Gerrighty's evidence that Ward responded to a personal request (made by the garda to his girlfriend Vanessa at his home) to telephone him. The sergeant told Ward that he was investigating the murder and asked him if he had any knowledge of it. Ward said that he was in his house with his niece and the investigator asked her name, saying he wanted to check Ward's alibi. Ward hung up without providing her name. It later emerged that she was Natasha Madden, a drug-addict who, Ward's defence team claimed, was being detoxed by Ward at his home.

Leahy then asked the court to consider the evidence of two detectives who interviewed Ward following his arrest on October 16, 1996. The court had heard that Ward told them of his girlfriend Vanessa: "She knows nothing. She wasn't in the house that day – the day the Guerin one was shot. She knows nothing."

Details were given of how Ward allegedly told the interviewers that two named gang members called to his house after the shooting: "Youse know why they called," he is said to have told them. "We planned after the job was done on Guerin that they would come back to my place. I was to get rid of them." By *them*, he meant *the gun and the bike*.

Evidence of a second interview the next day was also proffered: "No, I am not saying any more. I was only asked to look after the bike and the gun." Referring to the gun, he added: "After the shooting it was left in my house. I had to get rid of the f**king thing." Adding of the bike: "I had to get that off-side too."

He is alleged to have said: "My part was to let them use my house after the shooting. They came with the bike and the gun." Leahy reminded the court that Ward told detectives that he would plead guilty to drugs and firearms charges, but "I won't take the murder rap".

Mr Leahy also reminded the court of the evidence provided by Gardaí of Ward's attempts to protect his girlfriend, Vanessa Meehan, from the Gardaí and of how he is said to have told them that a named gang member "will go crazy if I involve her. She wasn't even in the house that day . . . f**k them. They didn't even ask if they could use my house".

"Ah for f**k's sake, leave it out, I have it up to here

with youse now . . . look, I have been asked over and over again about this poxy murder. I had nothing to do with it," Paul Ward is alleged to have said in a subsequent interview.

The evidence supplied by the supergrass Charles Bowden should also be considered as evidence of Ward's involvement, Mr Leahy said. He recalled Bowden's evidence of Ward's presence when conversations occurred regarding an assault case which Veronica planned to take against the gang leader. Mr Leahy referred to Bowden's evidence that a named gang member said in one of the conversations that the gang leader was the only person who knew the contacts for importing drugs into Ireland and that he was "completely pissed off" about the case.

The court should also accept Bowden's evidence that he met with Paul Ward in his Walkinstown house in the days following the murder and how Ward allegedly told Bowden that the assassin left the gun in his house. Mr Leahy said it was the State's submission that Bowden's evidence constituted a definite, prearranged killing.

He added, however, that the telephone evidence against Ward stands alone as a pillar with which to convict the accused of murder. Outlining this evidence, Mr Leahy gave details of four calls made from a gang member's mobile phone to Paul Ward's landline at Walkinstown Road which was in the name of his mother, Elizabeth.

Details were then given of a further six telephone calls made by the gang member from his mobile to Ward's mobile.

A further nine calls were made from Ward's mobile to the same gang member's mobile.

Mr Leahy reminded the court that the murder occurred at 12.55 p.m. (many of the calls were made in and around that time) and this was part of other evidence which was capable of supporting, not corroborating, the evidence provided by Charles Bowden.

While the prosecution decided to present the four pillars of their case, the defence – represented by Patrick McEntee – was not only determined to tear those pillars down but was setting no time limit.

From the opening submission 30 days before, Mr McEntee gave warning that his team would contest the alleged admissions by Ward while in custody, the mobile phone evidence and particularly the evidence of supergrass Charles Bowden who implicated Ward in the planning of the murder and disposal of the weapon and motorbike. Despite a tongue-lashing from Mr Justice Barr (over his inference that the state were not treating defence witnesses with respect) before beginning his opening remarks on Thursday, the legendary senior counsel was not shy in reminding the court of its obligations – as well as pointing out the fact that the prosecution must prove its case beyond reasonable doubt – and he urged the judges not to let the emotive elements of the murder invade their deliberations.

He asked the court to consider the context of the arrest. Ms Guerin had been assassinated in June and by October all of the big people had disappeared out of the country. It was reasonable to assume that when Bowden was arrested and started talking that the investigating team would go into top gear, and this made it essential for the Gardaí to make arrests.

In the counsel's view this is a stripped-down case and depends on a series of alleged verbal statements and the word of an informer. Taking the word of an informer was a very risky and dangerous basis for any case, and Mr McEntee cited the Diplock Courts' history of dealing with supergrasses, particularly the famous case of the prosecution of Gerard Steensen which collapsed when the Appeal Court rejected the evidence of the informer Kirkpatrick.

He said the supergrass was a deeply suspicious witness because he had inside knowledge from being involved in the criminal activities and could use that knowledge not in the interest of justice but in self-interest. Having been promised immunity, he must square up to his future as he sees it.

Mr McEntee then spoke about the general dangers of the case with respect to the fact that there was no jury. "Grave dangers have to be guarded against that might influence your Lords at unconscious or intuitive level," he boomed.

The judges were listening but he seemed to be preaching to the legally converted. The previously contested confidential material which the Supreme Court ruled was not to be shown to the defence was brought up, and while he did not know if it was prejudicial to his client, he said that it could, without their lordships realising it, influence them and they should put it from their minds. There was no evidence, he claimed, linking any members of the gang with the offence. The case was run by the prosecution on the narrowest possible basis, he said.

The prosecution did not attempt to show it was possible for the motorbike to get from the scene of the crime to Ward's house and then have two of the gang members who carried out the killing back into Moore Street for 1.30 p.m. (Then again neither did the defence attempt to prove that it was impossible.) He claimed that there was a major difficulty if the mobile phone calls were not made by the people in whose names the phones were registered. He said that the calls to and from the gang member who was on the motorbike were not proved to be possible given the circumstances of driving the bike. There was no evidence offered by the prosecution to say that it was possible. (But neither had the defence attempted to prove it was impossible.)

Mr McEntee then complained that while videos were available in many police stations there was none at Lucan, where the murder investigation was based. A video recording would have cleared up the matter of the two other pillars of evidence – the contested admissions made by Ward while in custody.

Mr McEntee would take all the next day, Friday, and the whole of Monday, the start of the eighth week and the 31st day of the trial to retrace all the evidence with meticulous care and attention to detail. At times this attention became tedious so that at one stage Mr Justice Robert Barr had to remind the counsel that he was not addressing a jury. By any standards it was a marathon address at the end of a process that began with the arrest of Paul Ward in October 1996 followed by two years of legal battle before the trial. Whatever the outcome, nobody could deny that the full defence and rigours of the law had been afforded the accused. At 37 minutes past five o clock on the evening of Monday November 23, 1998 the trial of Paul Ward ended. Mr Justice Barr told the packed assembly that judgment would not be given before 2pm on Wednesday but the most experienced court reporter present, Diarmuid McDermott, predicted rightly it would not be delivered until Friday. He was right about two things – the timing of the judgment and the verdict. Those of less experience and even those close to the case would spend a nerve-wracking three days until the clerk announced time of delivery – Friday morning. A lot of us were numb after 31 days but as the time wore on towards Friday the adrenalin level began to pump very rapidly.

The feeling among reporters and observers and police the night before was in general pessimistic. To people I knew I urged a prayer but in my heart of hearts I knew that it would work out in the end. It did not stop a bout of the jitters which persisted all through Thursday and Friday. I joined the throng in the court and noticed many new faces. The Ward family occupied their usual place in the upper gallery as did Graham and Jimmy in opposite lower galleries. I managed to squeeze into the right-hand side of the lower gallery. I was paralysed with nervousness but tried to hide it. I opened my notebook and wrote on the top of the page *Judgment Day*. The impact of that title burned in my mind and sent me into a spiral. I tried to apply cold logic and calm. All through the complicated process of bringing Paul Ward to trial, the prosecution had cleared every legal hurdle. It was inconceivable that the case would fall at the last fence. I revived a bit and scanned the court. The upper gallery was occupied by journalists, the Ward family and members of the legal profession. On the extreme left, Aenghus Fanning editor of *The Sunday Independent*. The floor of the court was as usual occupied by the legal teams and the very last bench by the press corps. As the clock struck 11am I took a long quiet breath. Just after the hour the accused, Paul Ward, sat in the front and assumed the impassive demeanour of a man who was a spectator rather than a participant in the proceedings. I thought of you, Graham, Cathal and your family, all they had been through; the anguish, the pain, the loss and the constant reminders of that fateful day. You and they above all deserved justice. Five minutes later the court rose as the three judges entered. Before they settled, the atmosphere was thick with tension. Presiding Judge Robert Barr placed the judgment before him and began to read in loud, clear and precise tone. For the next 90 minutes my heart sank and rose and sank again like a small boat in high seas and my nerves crashed like waves against a rocky shoreline.

This is what Mr Justice Robert Bank read on that historic morning:

On 26th June, 1996 Ms Veronica Guerin, a distinguished and brave journalist who specialised in the investigation of crime, was brutally murdered when riddled with bullets as she sat in her car waiting for traffic-lights to change at the Naas Road, Boot Road junction, Clondalkin, Dublin. Eyewitnesses have established that as the victim waited at the lights a motorcycle on which there were two persons drew up alongside. The pillion passenger broke a window in the driver's door and then fired six bullets at point-blank range into the car. All struck the victim and caused fatal injuries from which it is probable that she died within seconds. Thereupon the motorcycle sped away and disappeared. The accused has been charged with the murder of Ms Guerin. The prosecution does not contend that he was the gunman or the motorcyclist or that he was present at the scene of the crime. The case against him is that he participated in the planning of the murder and that pursuant to such plans he played an important role in the crime by receiving from the killers very soon after the event the motorcycle and the gun which they had used and he disposed of both thereafter. The evidence against the accused comprises verbal admissions allegedly made by him while in police custody following his arrest under Section 30 of the Offences Against the State Act, 1939 on 16th October, 1996 and the testimony of Charles Bowden, an accomplice, whose evidence purports to establish that the accused was an accessory before the fact of Ms Guerin's murder.

The Verbal Admissions [Alleged to have been made by the Accused]

The accused was arrested at 3.30pm on 16th October, 1996 at Windmill Park, Crumlin, by Inspector (then Sergeant) Pádraig Kennedy and he was brought to Lucan Garda Station which was the headquarters of the Guerin murder investigation, one of the biggest ever mounted by the Garda Síochána. The accused is an experienced Section 30 detainee having been arrested on that basis on earlier occasions and he stated in evidence that he was well aware of the importance in his own interest of adopting a policy of total silence in course of interrogation and he alleged that he did so. He took two precautions on arrival at the station. He asked to see his solicitor and also a doctor. Shortly afterwards he had a consultation with his solicitor, Mr Hanahoe, who advised him of his right to silence and not to answer any questions. Dr Lionel Williams, a police doctor, examined him. The accused has stated that he had two reasons for asking for a doctor. First, he wished to be medically examined so that there would be, if necessary, professional evidence to establish that at the time of examination he bore no signs of physical injury. He deposed that the second reason was that he then and had been for some time a heroin abuser and he required a medication called physeptone to counter the symptoms of his alleged addiction. Dr. Williams did not regard him as being then in withdrawal but provided a single dose of physeptone to the police for the benefit of the accused should he require it. There is some controversy as to when and in what circumstances he received the medication.

The accused was interviewed by Detective Sergeant Kennedy and Detective Garda Curran from 4.10 to 4.25pm on the day of arrest (16th October). The next interview was from 7.15pm to 9.10pm conducted by Detective Sergeant Healy and Detective Garda Clancy. The third and final interview that day was by Detective Gardaí Byrne and Hanley from 9.55pm to 11.45pm.

On the following day the first interrogation session was with Detective Gardaí Dillon and O'Shea from 8.20am until 12.15pm, Detective Sergeant Lynagh having replaced Detective Garda O'Shea at 11.30am. The next session was with Detective Gardaí Hanley and O'Shea and it commenced at 2.25pm. It was interrupted by a visit from Mr Hanahoe from 3.00 to 3.10pm and for the reading of the Extension Order by the station sergeant at 3.20pm. There was also a short visit by Detective Sergeant Ennis of the Ballistics Section. The accused was returned to his cell from the interview room at 5.55pm. The next session was conducted by Detective Sergeant Lynagh and Detective Garda Dillon. It commenced at 7.35pm and was interrupted by a meeting between the accused and his partner, Ms. Vanessa Meehan, which took place in a different interview room. The visit was supervised by Detective Garda Hanley and lasted until 10.35pm when the accused was returned to the original interview room where the interrogation by Detective Sergeant Lynagh and Detective Garda Dillon continued until 11.25pm when the accused was returned to his cell for the night. There is controversy about an alleged nocturnal visit by Detective Garda Condon to the cell that night and it ultimately emerged in evidence and the court accepts that a noisy tattooed drunk was detained in the accused's cell for about 50 minutes in the early hours of the morning.

It is common case that until the accused's meeting with Ms Meehan the position was that in the course of five sessions comprising a total of fourteen hours of intense interrogation by a series of experienced police officers, the accused firmly maintained his policy of silence. On the premise that the evidence of Sergeant Lynagh and Garda Dillon is truthful, a profound change took place after that visit and admissions were made by the accused amounting to a confession of participation in the murder of Ms Guerin. It is alleged that the following admissions were made by the accused when his interrogation was continued by Sergeant Lynagh and Garda Dillon from 10.35pm. The interviewers contend that Garda Dillon recorded at the time the following questions and answers made thereto by the accused:-

"Prisoner visited girlfriend, Vanessa, at 10.25pm. Prisoner returned to Interview Room at 10.35pm.

Q.   What did Vanessa say to you?

A.   She knows nothing, she wasn't in the house that day.

Q.   What day?

A.   The day the Guerin one was shot. She wasn't in the house. She knows nothing about it.

Q.   What happened at your house after the shooting?

A.   (named gang members) called.

Q.   Why did they call to your house?

A.   You'se know why they called.

Q.   Tell us why?

A.   We had it planned after the job was done on Guerin they would come back to my place, I was to get rid of the gear.

Q.   Why do you mean by gear?

A.   The gun and the bike, I got rid of them.

Q.   Where are they now?

A.   No response.

Q.   Is it hidden where someone else will find it? You know someone else might get shot?

A.   No response.

A number of other questions are recorded as having been asked and in each case it is noted that there was no response.

This poses two alternative possibilities. If the alleged admissions were made then, they constituted a huge breakthrough in the Guerin investigation. What was said clearly amounted to admissions by the accused that he was guilty of being an accessory before the fact of murder and thus in law would be as guilty as the actual participators i.e. the gunman and the motorcyclist. The accused was the first person, other than Charles Bowden, to confess to participation in the murder of Ms Guerin. The police were under severe pressure to bring charges in regard to that crime. The coincidence that the accused's capitulation after more than fourteen hours of silence during interrogations had occurred immediately after the visit by Ms Meehan is a remarkable *volte face* which gives rise to unease and raises a series of pertinent questions. Why did that visit take place? What was its real motivation? What transpired between the accused and his partner on that occasion? What was Ms Meehan's state of mind at the time? Was she pressurised by the police in any way to attempt to break down the accused's resolve to maintain silence and to persuade him to make admissions about his involvement in the crime? In reality, was the first visit a deliberate ploy devised by the police to soften up the accused and cause him to incriminate himself as to the murder?

Ms Meehan was arrested under Section 30 of the 1939 Act at 6.55pm on 16th October and was detained at Ballyfermot Garda Station where she was interviewed by Detective Sergeant Kennedy. She made a written statement to the effect that she was at home with the accused on the day of the murder until late afternoon when she went to her mother's house. She described that the accused's niece, Natasha Madden, was also staying in the house at the time. The latter had been brought there on the previous day suffering from grievous heroin addiction. She explained in evidence that the accused had agreed to take Natasha in and look after her. This included providing physeptone which was obtained and administered to her by the accused. Her statement is silent on whether there were any visitors to the house that day but in her evidence she denied that anyone had called. The accused's testimony had been to the same effect. She said that in the course of interrogations police officers had shouted at her and threatened to have her charged as an accessory to murder. They did not believe that she was in the house on the day of the murder at the relevant time when they contended that the motorcycle and gun were delivered to the accused. However, she did not change her statement at that time though she alleged that she was crying and very distressed during her stay at Ballyfermot station. She did not ask to visit the accused. Nevertheless, on the evening of 17th October, she was brought to Lucan station where she arrived at 8.40pm. Shortly afterwards she was taken to an interview room where she was interrogated by Detective Gardaí O'Shea and Hanley from 8.50 to 10.07pm. She described her situation at that time as being very upset and frightened and she was crying a lot. The interrogators referred to her earlier statement about being in the house at the material time on 26th June and she was again threatened with being charged as an accessory to murder. She was told that the charge sheet was being prepared and the charge would proceed if she did not change her statement by saying that she left the house earlier in the morning. Ms Meehan was asked by Mr McEntee about the circumstances of her encounter with the accused at Lucan Garda Station. The following passage is recorded in Volume 26 of the transcript of evidence at pp 25/6:-

"A. Well, the detectives were saying to me we are going to bring you in to see Paul now and you ask him where the gun is, because if you ask him that, we will let you go home and we will let Paul go home if Paul tells us where the gun is. So they brought me into a room.

Q. Did you ask to see Paul?

A. No.

Q. And did you believe that if you were to get Paul to divulge where they maintained the gun was that he would be let home?

A. I was just – I was more concerned about myself to be honest. I just wanted to get out of the police station and they said if I did this and if I asked him, that they would let me go and they would let Paul go, but I wasn't really too concerned about Paul at that stage to be honest.

Q. Yes. So tell their Lordships what happened then.

A. So they brought me into a room.

Q. From where?

A. From where they were after being interviewing me, they brought me to a different room.

Q. From another room where they had been interviewing you?

A. Yes. I was sitting at the edge of a table, and out in the hallway I could hear a commotion and I could – the door was open and I could just see the corner of Paul's, you know, his shoulder and they were, as far as I remember, they were screaming at him to go into the room and Paul wasn't coming into the room.

Q. Did you hear Paul say anything at that stage?

A. I couldn't clearly hear what they were saying and I was crying and I called out to Paul.

Q. What did you call out?

A.   Just to come in.

Q.   Did he come in?

A.   Yes.

Q.   What happened?

A.   I was, I was very upset and I was asking him just to, I asked him to tell them where the gun was so that I could go home and he was saying like he had nothing got to do with it and he was saying, you know I haven't anything to do with it and I was just saying well, they just said if I asked you they would let me go home and then Paul asked me what time I was after being arrested at and I told him and he said that he was after being arrested earlier than me, so he said "I will be out before you" and he said "I will be out before you and I will collect you."

Q.   What happened then?

A.   They took Paul back out of the room then and I can't remember whether I was put into a cell straight after it or whether they questioned me, I am not too sure, but I said it to him, I said they asked me what did Paul say.

Q.   Were there guards present when you talked to Paul?

A.   No.

Q.   Yes.

A.   And they asked me what did Paul say so I said I am after asking him and he has nothing got to do with it and I said can I go now because I am after doing what you asked me to. They just started laughing.

Q.   When you went in to see Paul or when Paul was brought in to see you in that room, did you at that stage know that the guards . . . what the guards were saying about the allegations about Paul's involvement in the matter?

A.   Yes, they had been saying it throughout the day.

Q.   What had they been saying?

A.   They were saying that he had got rid of the gun and the motorbike as well.

In the course of her interrogation by Garda Hanley and O'Shea prior to her meeting with the accused she said that they concentrated on her partner's involvement with the gun and said that he was going to go down for 20 years. They also kept insisting that Shay Ward had been in the house that day, which she denied. Eventually she was prevailed on to make a new written statement in which under severe pressure she agreed to change what she had said originally and to concede that she had left the house in the morning and was not present at the material time on 26th June. She said that she signed a statement to that effect.

Garda (now Sergeant) Hanley and Inspector Kennedy were unable to provide any credible explanation as to why it was deemed necessary and appropriate to interrogate Ms Meehan for an hour and a quarter just before her meeting with the accused. There was also no tenable explanation as to why the meeting had taken place and why Ms Meehan was kept in a cell at Lucan Garda Station that night instead of being returned to Ballyfermot Station.

The history of the accused's interrogation on 18th October as conceded by the relevant police witnesses is very remarkable indeed. Notwithstanding the accused's alleged positive verbal admission after the Vanessa meeting that he was an accessory before the fact to the murder of Ms Guerin, the first two teams of interrogators who questioned the accused for a total of almost two hours between them on that morning were not aware of what the accused is alleged to have admitted to Sergeant Lynagh and Garda Dillon on the previous night and had no knowledge of the crucial memorandum which had been made in that regard. This indicates either incredible disorganisation in the murder investigation despite the fact that there was a continuously manned Incident Room at Lucan station, or there was no memorandum of the Lynagh/Dillon interview at that time and it came into existence later. That possibility would explain another problem which has not been fully addressed by the prosecution. The accused requested a visit from Dr Williams which took place at 2.44pm on that day. The latter gave evidence that he saw an obvious red mark by way of injury on the accused's neck at that time. It was not there when the doctor originally examined the accused. The explanation given by the latter is that it was caused by Sergeant Condon in course of the first interview that day which is referred to in the ruling by the Court on the *voir dire*. Sergeant Condon denies the accused's allegations against him but no evidence has been adduced by the prosecution about how the mark on the accused's neck came to be there. In particular, it was not suggested in cross-examination that it has been self-inflicted. If the prosecution case is correct there would be no possible reason for an assault on the accused after he had made a positive confession of guilt on the previous night. An assault by Sergeant Condon is, however, consistent with the accused's contention that he maintained silence and admitted nothing during the period of his detention. Was Sergeant Condon responsible for an attempted physical softening up of the accused because the Vanessa Meehan stratagem had failed?

Detective Sergeant Hanley commenced an interview with the accused at 10.50am and he was joined five minutes later by Detective Garda O'Shea. They appear to have been the first interviewing officers that day who were aware of the alleged crucial admissions made by the accused on the previous night. He was cautioned and early in the interview the accused asked if Vanessa was still in custody and added that she knew nothing and asked Sergeant Hanley to let her go. When Garda O'Shea arrived he said, "You have started to tell the truth, tell us all you know about it." The accused then repeated admissions broadly similar to those he is recorded as having had made on the previous night. In particular he is alleged to have said "My part was to let them use my house after the shooting, they came with the bike and the gun." He is also alleged to have conceded that he had a scanner and that he heard the call going out about the shooting on the Naas Road. He knew then that the bike would be arriving. It was put in his garage and he would not say anything else about it. He did not respond to questions about the murder weapon. It will be appreciated from the foregoing that there was some reference by Detective Garda O'Shea to the admissions allegedly made by the accused on the previous night.

It is contended that similar admissions as to the accused's involvement were made by him to Detective Sergeant Healy and Detective Garda Clancy at an interview which commenced at 1.52pm on 18th October. On that occasion his explanation for agreeing to take charge of the motorcycle and the gun after the shooting was stated to be that he was a "junkie" and needed the money which had been promised to him for agreeing to perform that service when the murder was being planned by the leader and his first lieutenant (named gang members).

After that interview another very disquieting episode took place. Mrs. Elizabeth Ward, a woman of 74 years of age, the accused's mother was also a detainee in garda custody at Cabra station consequent upon her arrest under Section 30. The court is satisfied that she did not ask to see her son and that he did not ask to see her. Nonetheless, she was brought to Lucan Garda Station where she arrived at 2.25pm on 18th October which was an hour and five minutes before the time when the accused would have to be charged or released from custody. The circumstances of her arrival at Lucan are most disturbing. Detective Gardaí Paul Gilton and Tony Ryan were deputed by a senior officer to interview Mrs Ward at Cabra station. When they arrived there at 2pm they were asked to convey the detainee to Lucan for the purpose of visiting her son. This request was made by Detective Garda Mary Murphy, a junior officer, and they immediately did what they were asked without reference to their superior officer or any other person in authority. Mrs Ward described the journey in course of her evidence in the *voir dire* in graphic terms. She was put into a police car and driven to Lucan at speed with siren blaring. She was terrified and pleaded with the driver to slow down but he didn't do so. The circumstances as described by Mrs Ward were not seriously challenged in the evidence of the officers concerned. It was also conceded that no steps were taken before the journey to ascertain whether it would be convenient to interrupt the interrogation of the accused for the purpose of a social visit from his mother or whether he was willing to accept such a visit. On arrival at Lucan all formalities were dispensed with and Mrs Ward's meeting with the accused took place within a minute or two of her arrival at the station. The accused was distressed by his mother's visit because he was concerned about her and about his aged father who was in poor health and who also was in Section 30 detention at the time. The interrogation session being carried out by Detective Sergeant Healy and Detective Garda Clancy was interrupted for the purpose of the meeting between mother and son which concluded at 2.43pm having commenced at 2.27pm. That visit was followed by a two-minute meeting between Dr Williams and the accused. The Healy/Clancy interrogation was resumed immediately thereafter. There was no caution at that time and the accused immediately complained that some Gardaí had told his mother that he was on gear i.e. was taking serious drugs. Detective Sergeant Healy's response was to deny that he or Garda Clancy had spoken to Mrs Ward and he said, "Let's get back to where you hid the gun. We want to find the gun so that nobody else will be killed with it." The accused replied, "Nobody will ever be killed by the gun where it is now." He was then asked, "Where did the gun come from?" And he replied, "You know well where it came from, it was with the guns and ammunition you got in the graveyard."

The Court is satisfied beyond all reasonable doubt that the visit from Mrs Ward was a deliberate ploy devised and orchestrated by the police in a final effort to prevail on the accused to disclose what he had done with the gun. It is obvious that if it had been possible to trace that weapon it might have yielded valuable forensic information which could have been helpful in establishing the guilt of others in addition to the accused. The Court is satisfied that the visit was not arranged for any humanitarian purpose but was a cynical ploy which it was hoped might break down the accused and cause him to make what was perceived to be a crucial admission regarding what had happened to the weapon.

As to the visit from Ms Vanessa Meehan to the accused; the Court accepts her evidence that she was successfully subjected to grievous psychological pressure by Detective Sergeant Hanley, and perhaps other officers also, to assist the police in breaking down the accused who up till then had maintained consistent silence over many interrogation sessions. Both meetings amounted to a conscious and deliberate disregard of the accused's basic constitutional right to fair procedures and treatment while in custody. They constituted deliberate gross violations of the fundamental obligation which the interrogators and their superiors had of conducting their dealings with the accused in accordance with principles of basic fairness and justice. Another alarming feature relating to events during the period of the accused's detention at Lucan Garda Station is the extraordinary fact that a number of significant documents are now alleged to be unaccountably missing. In all the circumstances the Court is satisfied that in the interest of justice and fairness all admissions allegedly made by the accused during the period of his detention at Lucan Garda Station must be ruled inadmissible.

The Court also has some element of doubt about whether the alleged verbal admissions were in fact made by the accused or whether, as he contends, he made no admissions at all during the entire period of his detention. There is some evidence which might reasonably be regarded as supporting the accused's denial of having made any admissions. Perhaps the most significant is the remarkable fact that the first two pairs of interrogators who interviewed the accused on 18th October were unaware of the fundamental breakthrough which is alleged to have occurred at the last interrogation session on the previous night when, it is contended, the accused in effect admitted to being an accessory before the fact of murder. It is incredible that these officers were unaware of the accused's confession if it had been made. The Court would have expected that at the first opportunity after that late-night admission the police would have been anxious to pursue the matter with the accused as soon as practicable with a view to obtaining further information from him. The unexplained absence of documents might have some relevance in that regard. The inquiry sustained by the accused while in custody is also supportive of the case which he has made. The Court is not making a finding that the verbal admissions were in fact planted by the police as alleged, but the evidence suggests such a possibility and the accused must be given the benefit of the element of doubt which exists. Accordingly, the admissibility of the alleged verbal admissions are excluded on that ground also.

In arriving at its decision to declare inadmissible the accused's alleged voluntary admissions to the police, the Court has had regard to the statement of law as to the assessment of alleged voluntary admissions made by the accused person contained in the following passage from the Supreme Court judgment of Griffin J, in The People - v - Shaw [1982]I.R. 1 at p.60/61:-

"The primary requirement is to show that the statement was voluntary, in the sense in which that adjective has been judicially construed in the decided cases. Thus, if the tendered statement was coerced or otherwise induced or extracted without the true and free will of its maker, it will not be held to have been voluntarily made. The circumstances which will make a statement inadmissible for lack of voluntariness are so varied that it would be impossible to enumerate or categorise them fully. It is sufficient to say that the decided cases show that a statement will be excluded as being involuntary if it was wrung from its maker by physical or psychological pressures, by threats or promises made by persons in authority, by use of drugs, hypnosis, intoxicating drink, by prolonged interrogation or excessive questioning, or by any one of a diversity of methods which have in common the result or the risk that what is tendered as a voluntary statement is not the natural emanation of a rational intellect and free will . . .

Secondly, even if a statement is held to have been voluntarily obtained in the sense indicated, it may nevertheless be inadmissible for another reason. Because our system of law is accusatorial and not inquisitorial, and because (as has been stated in a number of decisions of this Court) our Constitution postulates the observance of basic or fundamental fairness of procedures, the judge presiding at a criminal trial should be astute to see that, although a statement may be technically voluntary, it should nevertheless be excluded if by reason of the manner of the circumstances in which it was obtained it falls below the required standards of fairness. The reason for exclusion here is not so much the risk of an erroneous conviction as the recognition that the minimum of essential standards must be observed in the administration of justice. Whether the objection to the statement may be unconstitutional or on other grounds, the crucial test is whether it was obtained in compliance with basic or fundamental fairness, and the trial judge will have a discretion to exclude it 'where it appears to him that public policy based on a balancing of public interests, requires such exclusion'. Per Kingsmill Moore J at p.161, The People - v - O'Brien [1965] I.R. 142 . . ."

The conduct of the police in devising and orchestrating the meetings between the accused and his partner, Ms Meehan, and subsequently with his mother amounted to psychological pressures as envisaged by Griffin J in Shaw's case. Such pressures amounted to a deliberate denial of fundamental fairness in the interrogation of the accused. It also raises the question of a balancing of public interests as envisaged by Kingsmill Moore J in O'Brien's case and justice requires that all incriminating statements alleged to have been made by the accused to the police in course of his interrogation should be declared inadmissible as evidence at the trial.

The Court also has been mindful of the following passage in the judgment of Finlay CJ for the Court of Criminal Appeal in The People - v - Burckley, delivered on 31st July, 1989 and reported in Frewen II p.210 at pp. 212/3:-

"The Court is satisfied that the cases to which reference

has been made would appear to establish a principle that where an accused person makes a statement which is incriminatory in nature and has previously been induced to make a statement either by promise, threat or oppression, also incriminatory in nature, which is by that fact rendered inadmissible, that the Court must in respect of the latter statement, even though no immediate circumstances of oppression, threat or inducement surrounded it, have regard to the possibility that the threat or inducement remains so as to affect the free will of the party concerned and, therefore, the voluntary nature of the statement."

The Court is satisfied beyond reasonable doubt that the alleged admissions made by the accused in course of his interrogation by Detective Sergeant Lynagh and Detective Garda Dillon on the night of 17th October (if in fact made by him) were induced by grievous psychological pressure, which emanated from his meeting with Ms Meehan immediately prior thereto, to such an extent that there was a real risk that the pressure remained and affected the free will of the accused to such a degree that it undermined the voluntary nature of subsequent alleged admissions made by him – if such were in fact made.

There is one other matter which the Court believes it is proper to comment upon. It emerged in course of the evidence given by Mr. Spencer, the ballistics expert, called on behalf of the accused, that he was accorded scant courtesy and there was lack of reasonable co-operation shown to him by Detective Sergeant Ennis when he visited the Ballistics Section for the purpose of examining and carrying out appropriate tests on various exhibits there. Detective Sergeant Ennis stated in evidence that he had instructions to provide only minimum assistance to Mr Spencer. Whoever was churlish enough to issue those instructions did a great disservice to an admirable unit of the Garda Síochána and in particular to Detective Sergeant Ennis whose outstanding service over many years has done so much to enhance the reputation of the Ballistics Section.

CHARLES BOWDEN

The second leg of the prosecution case against the accused is the evidence of Charles Bowden, an admitted accomplice in the murder of Ms Guerin, who also implicates the accused as one of those who participated in the planning of the murder and who he alleges in accordance with that plan provided a crucial back-up service for the actual killers by taking charge of the motorcycle and the gun used in the crime at his home, 113 Walkinstown Road, soon after the event and by subsequently disposing of both. What may have been the motorcycle in question was later found broken up in the River Liffey, but the gun was never found and no information emerged at the trial as to what became of it. There is no doubt that at all times the gardaí have been most anxious to trace the weapon.

The first question the Court must address in assessing the credibility of Bowden is his status in the case. Is he no more and no less than a self-confessed accomplice in the murder of Ms Guerin or is he one of a category of accomplices as found in certain terrorist trials in the Diplock courts of Northern Ireland known as a "supergrass" such as Henry Kirkpatrick in the last of such trials – see The Queen - v - Steenson & Ors., [1986] 17

NIBJ36. Mr McEntee contends that Bowden is in the same category as Kirkpatrick; that his evidence should be approached by the court with even greater reserve and suspicion than that of an ordinary accomplice and that for reasons similar to those advanced by the Lord Chief Justice of Northern Ireland, Lord Lowry, vis-a-vis Kirkpatrick in the Steenson case, Bowden's evidence should be rejected by the court as utterly unreliable.

Lord Lowry LCJ in the course of his judgment in the Northern Ireland Court of Appeal in Steenson's case at page 45 quoted with approval the following passage from the judgment of Hutton in R - v - Crumley, [1984] unreported, which was also a supergrass case:-

"It is essential for a judge to warn a jury (and to remember, if he is the tribunal of fact) that it is dangerous to convict any accused on any count of an indictment on the evidence of an accomplice, if uncorroborated as to that accused and as to that count. But a supergrass is no ordinary criminal and no ordinary accomplice. Therefore, to the extent that what is known about the supergrass's character and situation increases the probability that he will be an unreliable witness, the danger of acting on his uncorroborated evidence is increased. In this case, as in so many similar cases, we are confronted with a witness who, by his own admission, was a man of lawless character, a member of an unlawful organisation dedicated to violence and to the principle that the end justifies any means, including indiscriminate murder, and a person who had wholeheartedly engaged in all the activities of that organisation. He is not just a cornered criminal, who is reluctantly disgorging information to save himself from enduring the penalty of perhaps one moderately serious crime, but he has volunteered a veritable mass of damning information against men whom he alleges have been his confederates, to whom and with whom he is bound by an oath to further a joint cause which he no doubt regarded as patriotic. His motive may be fear, despair or hope of an enormously improved life for the future, or a mixture of the three: wherever the truth lies, his motive is extremely powerful. It is manifest that the evidence of such a witness must stand up successfully to the sternest criteria before it can be acceptable and become the sole basis for being satisfied beyond reasonable doubt that any accused is guilty of any offence charged against him."

This Court is satisfied that Charles Bowden is not a supergrass in the sense envisaged by Hutton LJ but when admitting his own part in the Guerin murder and in implicating others in that crime, including the accused, he furnished information to the police as a cornered criminal to extricate himself in part at least from a grievous situation in which he found himself. The Court is deeply mindful of the fundamental principle of criminal law that it is unsafe to act upon the evidence of an accomplice which is not corroborated in some material particular implicating the accused. This principle is laid down in the judgment of Kingsmill Moore J for the Supreme Court in People - v - Casey No. II, [1963] 33 at p.37.

The law as to the ingredients required to sustain a conviction of a person accused as an accessory before the fact for aiding and abetting in the commission of a murder is laid down in the judgment of O'Higgins CJ for the Court of Appeal in The People - v - Madden, [1977] I.R.336 at 340/341 as follows:-

"In the absence of evidence showing that any one of the accused actually took part in the shooting of Laurence White, the case made against each of them is that he aided and abetted in the killing of the deceased. The killing of the deceased is described in the evidence which undoubtedly establishes that it was accomplished in a manner from which the *mens rea* required for the offence of murder may be inferred in relation to the persons by whom the killing was committed. To sustain a conviction of any one of the accused as an accessory before the fact for aiding and abetting in the commission of his crime, the prosecution must prove that the acts of aiding and abetting attributed to the accused were done in the knowledge of the intended commission, and assisted the commission, of the actions carrying the *mens rea* of the offence committed by the principal, that is to say, an unlawful killing such as is described in section 4, sub-section (1) of the Criminal Justice Act, 1964. It is not contested that the trial court correctly stated the principles of law in relation to the onus of proof on the part of the prosecution to establish the guilt of a person accused of aiding and abetting the commission of the offence charged. The court has regard to the decision of the Court of Criminal Appeal in England in R - v - Bainbridge, [1960] 1 Q.B. 129 in which Lord Parker CJ quotes with approval the charge to a jury given by a trial judge in that case as set out at pp. 132 and 133 of the report. The court had regard also to the decision of the Queen's Bench Division in England in National Coal Board - v - Gamble, [1959] 1 Q.B.11 and, in particular to the statement of principle extracted from the judgment of Devlin J at pp. 20 and 23 of that report. The objection taken on the appeal is not that the trial court mis-stated the principles of law but that, in the application therefore, the court misdirected itself in relation to the evidence before it.

In relation to a charge of aiding and abetting, it is clear from the cited judgments in Bainbridge's case and Gamble's case that motives and desires are irrelevant, and that mere evidence of common association is insufficient. The kernel of the matter is the establishing of an activity on the part of the accused from which his intentions may be inferred and the effect of which is to assist the principal in the commission of the crime proved to have been committed by the principal, or the commission of a crime of a similar nature known to the accused to be the intention of the principal when assisting him."

There is no doubt that the killing of Ms Guerin falls squarely within the definition of murder as stated in Section 4 of the Criminal Justice Act, 1964. The court has also no hesitation in concluding that if it is established by admissible evidence that the accused participated in the planning of that crime and as part of that plan agreed to take responsibility for disposal of the motorcycle and/or gun used in the crime and in fact did so he is an accessory before the fact of the murder of Ms Guerin.

The Court accepts without any doubt that Charles Bowden is a self-serving, deeply avaricious and potentially vicious criminal. On his own admission he is a liar and the Court readily accepts that he would lie without hesitation and regardless of the consequences for others if he perceived it to be in his own interest to do so. The Court fully appreciates that assessment of his evidence must be made with great caution and with the foregoing firmly in mind.

After his arrest under Section 30 of the Offences Against the State Act, 1939 on 5th October, 1996 Bowden was detained in custody for 48 hours and was repeatedly interrogated by Garda investigators. Originally, he told them what he admitted in evidence at this trial was a tissue of lies. Later, he started to tell what he now deposes is the truth about the crime and the background to it. By degrees the whole story emerged in the course of his interrogation. However, even after he embarked on his confession, he was inconsistent in what he said to various officers. His explanation in that regard has an element of credibility. He says that he trusted some officers such as Inspector O'Mahony and Detective Sergeant Hanley, to whom most admissions were made, and he distrusted others.

However, the reason advanced by Bowden for his sudden decision to tell the truth about the murder and its background borders on the absurd and is totally rejected by the Court. He has stated in evidence that he was shown photographs by Detective Sergeant McCartan of the victim lying on a dissecting table with bullet holes in her body. He went on to say that later when alone he saw the same scene in his mind's eye but with his own wife's face substituted for that of the victim. He contends that this caused him to be overcome with shame and remorse for having played any part in the crime and for that reason he decided to confess all. The Court is satisfied that Mr Bowden is not the sort of man to have been overcome with grief or remorse about the killing of Ms Guerin. On the contrary, like other senior members of [named leader's] gang he had good reason to welcome her death, whoever her assassins may have been, bearing in mind that his leader [named gang leader] the lynch-pin in a major criminal business enterprise, faced a probable jail term on Ms Guerin's account which was likely to cripple the business for the period of his enforced absence to the great detriment of all, including his lieutenant, Bowden. The Court accepts the evidence of Mr Senan Moloney, Bowden's next-door neighbour, which to some extent was corroborated by the latter, that there was a raucous party in his house which lasted through most of the night of 26th/27th June, 1996. It seems that there was no remorse but plenty of celebration at the Bowden home that night, though it is fair to add that Mr Moloney also said that it was not a once-off event but a frequent occurrence there.

Mr Bowden is an intelligent man. The Court is satisfied that the reason for his conversion to the alleged truth had nothing to do with remorse as he contends but is the produce of a cold dispassionate assessment of his grievous situation at that time and amounted to a decision on his part to extricate himself as best he could from what he probably perceived to be the reality of his situation then. The police had discovered, or were about to discover, that he had possession or control of very large sums of money which established his status as a major player in the marketing of huge quantities of cannabis. The net was closing in. His involvement as tenant of the premises at Harold's Cross, used for storage and distribution of the cannabis and containing a large quantity of the product, had emerged. It was enough to make almost half a million cannabis cigarettes. Worst of all, some other gang member might inform on him and tell the police about his involvement in cleaning and loading the murder weapon for use in the crime thus rendering him guilty of murder as an accessory before the fact. The Court is satisfied that Bowden was motivated by self-interest in voluntarily admitting his own involvement and that of others in the murder of Ms Guerin. The conclusion is inescapable that he would have perceived himself as being at high risk of conviction for the murder of Ms Guerin; that all his money would be lost and that after conviction his bargaining position might very well be reduced to zero. He had every reason to seek to bail himself out of that dreadful situation as best he could and soon. He did so. He had agreed to turn state evidence in this and other related trials in return for a written undertaking from the Director of Public Prosecutions not to prosecute him for the murder of Ms Guerin. He has also obtained modest prison sentences having pleaded guilty to major drugs and arms crimes. He has secured concessions while in prison and his wife and children have been given the benefit of the Witness Protection Programme. Although not yet finally negotiated, it seems likely that when Bowden serves his sentence or earlier he will be released and set up with a new identity in a foreign country and some money in lieu of his substantial ill-gotten gains will be provided for him. It seems that he has made what, from his perspective, appears to have been probably the best bargain he could hope to achieve from the State in all the circumstances.

However, there is no doubt that Bowden would also appreciate that to achieve the foregoing advantages it would be in his best interest to tell the truth about all relevant details known to him relating to the murder and also [named gang leader's] criminal business enterprise. He is clever enough to realise and he has been told in terms that the information he furnished would be thoroughly checked out. He knows that if he is found to be lying as to any material fact much of the situation he has salvaged for himself and his family may be jeopardised. The Court accepts that Bowden is fully aware that it is in his best interest to tell the truth about those involved in the murder and that he is likely to have done so unless on any issue crucial to the case against the accused, Paul Ward, it appeared to him, Bowden, that it was or might be in his interest to lie and wrongly implicate the accused. If, in assessing the evidence, the Court has a reasonable doubt that that might be so then Bowden's evidence against the accused would be fatally flawed and would have to be rejected. In the final analysis, that is the net issue in this case.

The evidence given by Bowden about [named gang leader's] business enterprise, and the major part played by him and others, including the accused and [named gang member] in it, has been corroborated and supported in its essentials by the accused in evidence. It seems, therefore, that he, Bowden, has told the truth about these matters.

Bowden has also made a full and frank confession about his involvement as the armourer for the gang and in particular the part he played in preparing and loading the gun used in the killing. Although he made some attempt to distance himself from specific knowledge of an intention to kill on the part of [named gang members] he conceded that he knew it was their intention to shoot Ms

Guerin. That knowledge would imply that the victim was at risk of death or grievous personal injury from the attack which would be sufficient to establish his guilt as an accessory before the fact of murder. That being so, it is essentially irrelevant to his already admitted guilt whether or not he was also involved in disposal of the gun after the crime.

It is suggested by Mr McEntee that Bowden implicated the accused and in particular cast him in the role of disposer of the gun so as to avoid having to admit to being the person actually responsible for so doing. As already pointed out, having admitted to his part in preparing and loading the gun, he had no incentive for not admitting to having disposed of it after the crime if that were the fact or the original intention of the planners. On the contrary, that is a piece of information which the police would have welcomed – particularly if it were possible to retrieve the weapon and have it forensically examined. There does not seem to be anything to suggest that falsely implicating the accused in the crime might have been of advantage to Bowden. His evidence already implicated [named gang members] who are those he alleges are primarily responsible for the murder. There are also other senior members of the gang he did not seek to implicate directly in the death of Ms Guerin, i.e. [named gang members]. There does not seem to be any tenable reason for singling the accused out as disposer of the gun and receiver of the motorcycle if that were untrue. It is suggested by Mr McEntee that as Bowden had professional knowledge of guns from his experience as a soldier, it is probable that at the planning stage he would have been made responsible not only for preparing and loading the gun but also for its disposal after the crime. It is entirely credible that such an arrangement might have been made. However, if it was made, a strong probability would be that Bowden by arrangement would have been in the accused's house at the time when two named gang members arrived and that he would have taken possession of the gun there. The shooter would have been anxious to get rid of it at the earliest possible opportunity and neither he or (named gang member) would have welcomed the idea of bringing it all the way to Bowden's hairdressing establishment in Moore Street with the attendant risk of being stopped and searched by the police as known drugs peddlers. The Court takes the view that it is not a credible possibility that [named gang member] would have walked from Aungier Street – where he was seen with [another named gang member] and identified by members of the Drugs Squad at about 1.30pm on the day of the murder – on through the inner city to Moore Street carrying the murder weapon, a bulky object which might have been mistaken for a consignment of cannabis by a vigilant policeman who would then arrest and search him. Such conduct would amount to a ridiculously foolhardy risk which could readily have been avoided by arranging with Bowden to hand over the gun to him at the accused's house immediately after the killing if the planners had decided that he, Bowden, should be responsible for disposal of the weapon. There are other credible reasons for [named gang members] meeting with Bowden at Moore Street, which appears to have taken place circa 1.40pm on 26th June. It may have been a drugs business encounter or an attempt by the former to set up an alibi.

The information furnished by Bowden to the police regarding the murder of Ms Guerin and the background to that crime are in two closely related parts. First, the background and motivation for the crime. The details he furnished in that regard may be summarised as follows:-

[Named gang member] was the leader and linchpin of a huge cannabis importing and distribution business in Ireland which also appears to have extended outside the State. Over a period in excess of two years up to June, 1996 over 100 metric tonnes of cannabis were imported into Ireland and subsequently distributed here and elsewhere. The turnover of the business during that period appears to have amounted to many millions of pounds. The cannabis arrived in one-kilo blocks. [Named gang leader] had five senior line managers who were responsible for receiving large on-going consignments of the drug which were delivered to one or more of them at a hotel premises in County Kildare. Each consignment was taken to a storage premises in Dublin which in May/June 1996 comprised a building in a commercial zone in Harold's Cross containing a few small industrial or manufacturing premises. There the consignments were divided up into lots ready for delivery to customers of the enterprise in accordance with the size of the orders received. The managers were [two named gang members] the accused, his brother and Charles Bowden who had been introduced in the group and recruited by [named gang member] for whom he had previously worked as a dealer in ecstasy tablets. Bowden's business acumen appears to have been recognised by the leadership. One of his functions was to negotiate rental agreements in connection with the store at Harold's Cross and earlier premises which had been used as depots by the gang. He also had a prominent role in preparing and distributing consignments of cannabis to wholesale customers mostly in large quantities on instructions from [two named gang members]. [Named gang member] assisted him in that end of the business. [Two named gang members] had responsibility for securing orders and arranging deliveries. The accused's primary function was to collect money owing by many customers for supplies received. According to his own evidence this was a more intricate operation than one would perceive at first sight. The going rate charged by [named gang leader's] business was £2,150 per kilo of cannabis. Wholesalers might place orders for upwards of £100,000 worth of the product. It was the practice not to discharge the debt in one cash payment but to divide it into as many as four payments to reduce the risk of loss. The accused described that all such payments would be made on behalf of the customer to him by arrangement in the course of the one day, usually in the carpark of a pub near his home. The accused would meet a courier for the customer who would hand him a plastic supermarket bag occasionally containing as much as £20,000 in cash. He would walk through the pub and out onto an adjacent street on the other side of the premises and then home to his house in Walkinstown Road. He often would make numerous such collections in the course of a day. At least once per week the cash collected by the managers was remitted to a courier for delivery to [named gang leader]. The latter received £2,000 per kilo sold and the balance of £150 per kilo was divided up among the five managers in equal shares. Their net earnings were in the region of £150,000 per annum each and probably substantially more. It was the practice of the management to hold a business meeting about once a week for the purpose of distributing their share of the profits. [Named gang leader] appears to have distanced himself from involvement in the distribution and marketing end of the business which he left in the hands of his five lieutenants. There was no evidence as to what his net profit would have been. It is reasonable to conclude that it was probably very substantial indeed.

Another feature of the business was that certain consignments of cannabis contained a substantial quantity of guns and ammunition which the gang stored in two graves in a Jewish cemetery near Tallaght. Covering slabs were removed; the arsenal was carefully stored in the graves underneath and the slabs were restored in their original positions. Subsequently, the police recovered the following from the graveyard:-

Five 9mm Walter semi-automatic pistols with silencers; a 9mm Sten sub-machine gun and silencer; a 9mm machine pistol and a large quantity of assorted ammunition for such weapons which included dum-dum and semi wad-cutter bullets. All were carefully stored in good condition and the witness appears to have had responsibility for so doing.

Bowden informed the police that [named gang leader] who was responsible for the importation of the cannabis also arranged for delivery of the guns and ammunition for use by the gang as and when required. This he did by arrangement with [named gang member]. The Court takes cognisance of the fact that major drug importation and wholesaling is a vicious business and in recent years numerous murders in Dublin have been associated with it.

As to motivation for the crimes; an incident had occurred between Ms Guerin and [named gang leader] it seems, in or about January, 1996 in which she had had an encounter with him and he had struck her. She reported the matter to the police and he was charged with assault. This enraged him because on imprisonment on foot of a likely jail sentence grave harm would be done to his cannabis empire because he would be prevented from purchasing supplies and arranging for the importation of the product into Ireland. It is also probable that he perceived himself as being hugely important in the criminal world and it would be a source of great annoyance and humiliation to be sent to jail as a petty criminal. It is also probable that his managers would have been also greatly annoyed by that turn of events. The end result was that a plot was hatched to murder Ms Guerin and thus the prosecution which she had initiated against [named gang leader] would have to be dropped as it was dependent on her evidence.

None of the foregoing information has been challenged by the accused and much of it was corroborated by him in course of his own evidence. He was entirely frank about his personal involvement as one of the five line managers for [named gang leader]. He also referred to a further piece of information which the Court has found most illuminating in corroborating Bowden's evidence about the background to, motivation for and the orchestration of the crime by the drugs godfather. In March 1996 a significant event took place at St Lucia in the West Indies. [Named gang member] and

Vanessa Meehan's sister were married there. This was a major social occasion for the Meehan family. Among other guests, [named gang member] attended; so did Vanessa Meehan with her partner, the accused, and most interestingly of all so did [named gang leader] and his wife. This event establishes the close connection between [named gang leader] and [named gang member] who appears to have been his senior manager and first lieutenant in crime. The accused was then close to the Meehan family, in particular this man and Vanessa. It is reasonable to conclude that [named gang leader] would have accepted him also as a trusted lieutenant. This is borne out by the fact that the accused appears to have been successful in having his brother taken on as one of the five managers. It is reasonable to assume that such an appointment would have required [named gang leader's] specific approval. It also emerged from the accused's evidence that in course of the wedding celebrations [named gang leader] expressed strong views about the assault charge brought by Ms Guerin. The accused deposed that this man had expressed the view that he would not be convicted. There was also some corroboration by Vanessa Meehan in that regard.

The end result is that up to that advanced point in the narrative relating to the murder of Ms Guerin, Charles Bowden appears to have been giving a truthful account of events which is substantially corroborated by or is unchallenged by the accused.

The remainder of Bowden's account concerns how he says the murder was planned and carried out. There were two prime performers. The first lieutenant who rode the motorcycle used in the event and a hired killer [named gang member], who when riding pillion on the motorcycle shot Ms Guerin at close range as she was stationary in her car just before 1pm on 26th June, 1996. The gun and bullets used were from the gang's arsenal in the cemetery. Bowden has also sought to establish that there were two subsidiary players on the murder team, both of whom had participated in the planning of the crime. He alleges that prior to its commission the first lieutenant had arranged that he and the accused would be responsible for collecting the gun and ammunition from the grave and the accused agreed to accept the motorcycle and the gun at his house in Walkinstown immediately after the crime and that he would take responsibility for disposing of both of them. The other person who Bowden named as an accessory before the fact of Ms Guerin's murder was himself. He admitted that he had an important function to play. It was his responsibility to clear and load the gun thus ensuring that it would be effective in bringing about the death of Ms Guerin. The Court takes cognisance of the fact that there is no evidence to suggest that he was obliged to make that admission. He could have relegated himself to the same status as the other business managers, [two named gang members] who are not directly implicated by him in the planning and execution of the crime.

Is it likely that Bowden has given a truthful account of the first lieutenant's involvement in the murder? The Court is satisfied that his evidence in that regard has a strong ring of truth about it. Bearing in mind the close connection between them and the first lieutenant's status in [named gang leader's] enormous drugs business, he is the person who would have been most likely to have been recruited by him to arrange the murder and also to participate by providing the transport which was crucial to success. The Court has no doubt that [named gang leader] would have welcomed the first lieutenant's presence as co-ordinator of the event to ensure that the gunman performed his duty. Is it likely that Bowden was truthful in naming this man as the gunman? Again, it is entirely credible that [named gang leader] would have arranged for the hiring of a professional killer to carry out the assassination. He would not have wanted a botched job. There is no evidence to suggest that any of his managers are professional killers but this man has that reputation. The crucial question then remains, was Bowden truthful in stating that the accused played a subsidiary part in the planning of the murder and in particular that prior thereto he adopted a crucial role as the person who would dispose of the motorcycle and the weapon used in the crime? Here again it is useful to hark back to [named gang leader]. He is the ultimate brains behind his extensive drugs business. There is every reason to believe that he orchestrated the killing of Ms Guerin. An important element in the transaction was immediate disposal of the motorcycle and gun. He would have realised that that function required to be in safe hands. Among his lieutenants the one who was closest to the first through family ties was the accused. A reasonable deduction from that relationship would be that the accused could be trusted to do the job. His performance as a collector of vast sums of money for [named gang leader] in course of business would emphasise the wisdom of entrusting him with that important function. The accused's house was also strategically placed and had the benefit of a discreet and secure garage. All in all, Bowden's evidence about the accused's involvement in the crime also has a strong ring of truth about it.

We come then to the question which is at the root of this case – is there any basis on which the court might reasonably suspect that Bowden had an interest to lie about the accused and wrongly implicate him in the crime of murdering Ms Guerin? As already stated, if in assessment of the evidence the Court has a reasonable doubt that that might be so then Bowden's evidence against the accused must be rejected. The Court can find nothing in the evidence which raises such a suspicion. If in fact Bowden had disposed of the gun, or prior to the crime had been deputed so to do, then, as previously stated, the strong probability is that he would have collected it at the accused's house. Furthermore, having admitted to preparing the gun for use in the killing, thus convicting himself of murder, it would have made no practical difference to admit to disposal of the weapon also if that were the case. The Court has carefully considered all of the evidence and can find nothing in it which might support a contention that Bowden had a motive of self-interest to implicate the accused in the crime. The Court also bears in mind that, apart from the gun, there was the question of disposal of the motorcycle. There is not the slightest suggestion that Bowden or anyone else other than the accused had responsibility in that regard. The Court is satisfied beyond reasonable doubt that Bowden's evidence implicating the accused in the crime is correct and ought to be accepted as truthful.

Mr McEntee has severely criticised Bowden's evidence

in a number of respects and it is proper that, insofar as it has not already done so in this judgment, the Court should comment on these submissions.

Mr McEntee referred to several alleged lies told by Bowden in evidence. All but one are minor matters of no significance in the case per se. The first relates to the witness's explanation for participating in named gang member's business relating to the distribution of ecstasy tablets. He referred to being "strapped for cash" through being behind in the rent and other expenses. In fact his employer provided him with accommodation for which he deducted the rent from wages. However, Bowden did explain that his marriage had broken down and he had substantial expenses in that regard. His reference to rent may not have been a lie in a conscious deliberate sense and could have been a casual inaccuracy. The second illustration relating to money which Bowden says he collected on a regular basis from a cannabis customer who lived nearby. He indicated that that was the only account he collected, but it transpired that a few of the first lieutenant's customers used to leave money occasionally at the hairdressing business for collection there. The Court does not consider that that amounted to a lie on the witness's part. The only account which he had personal responsibility for collecting was that of the customer in Blanchardstown who lived near Bowden's home.

Mr McEntee's main complaint relates to some confusion in Bowden's evidence as to whether the accused was present in the Hole in the Wall pub on the evening of the murder along with a number of other friends and associates including the first lieutenant. The witness did not state in evidence nor in any of his statements to the police that the accused was one of those who attended what appears to have been some form of party in Bowden's house late that night. Even if he had said so it would have had little or no significance in the context of the allegations made about the accused's alleged participation as a planner of the murder and provider of an important back-up service.

Bowden did tell lies about his proposed trip to London on which he was ready to embark at the time of his arrest. However, that is a matter on which he had an obvious interest in so doing and, as stated already, the Court has no doubt whatever he would probably tell lies where he perceived it to be in his interest so to do.

Mr McEntee has attached great significance to what he perceives to be lies told by Bowden about the bullets used in the killing. The court has no doubt whatever that all of the bullets fired by the gunman on the fatal occasion came from the store of bullets which the gang had at its disposal in the graveyard and that the gun came from there also. There is no reason whatever to disbelieve Bowden's admission that he was responsible for cleaning the gun, loading it and leaving it ready for murder. Much play has been made of some confusion in the witness's evidence about the bullets placed by him in the gun. He described them as being lead bullets inserted in cartridge cases but without the usual pointed tip. He said that the tip of each bullet was concave in profile and he provided the police with a rough line drawing illustrating what he meant. The Court is satisfied that the drawing illustrates what he described i.e. a concave tip when the bullet is looked at sideways on. His description does not accord with that of a dum-dum bullet which is not concave but which has a deep narrow hole in the centre of the flat top which is not visible sideways on. Ballistics evidence has established that the bullets fired by the gunman were the type known as semi wad-cutters. These are the same as dum-dum bullets but the top is solidly flat and there is no hole therein. Both types of bullet are suitable for use in 9mm pistols such as those found in the graveyard. The ammunition found there included dum-dum and semi wad-cutter bullets. The Court has examined a specimen of each. They are both of identical size fitted to similar metal casings. In profile they look the same but neither has a concave head. The description of the bullets which he inserted in the gun as given by the witness is slightly inaccurate but the Court attaches no significance to that error. There is no evidence that Bowden would have encountered either type of bullet in the course of his career in the army and it is of interest that the ballistics experts have stated in evidence that semi wad-cutters are used by sporting clubs for target practice. Surprisingly, it seems that they make a better hole in the target than pointed bullets of the type normally associated with military use.

Mr McEntee has also commented about what he perceives to be a shifting around in time and place of certain meetings alleged by the witness. The Court does not attach sinister significance to that contention and notes that in course of evidence the witness stated (see Book 23, pages 28/29) that it was not a case of moving one conversation to the other-

"It is the same subject being discussed in different places."

It is also submitted on behalf of the accused that his alleged confession to Bowden on 28th June at the accused's house (a meeting which he has stated never took place) is totally without context. Bowden's evidence in that regard is that he went to the accused's dwelling and had a conversation along with him there in course of which the accused is alleged to have told him about his part in the killing of Ms Guerin. He is criticised for not having said why he was there or what arrangements (if any) he had made to meet the accused at that time. It is true that no such explanation was given but it is credible that senior criminal business associates who on Bowden's evidence were both involved in the killing of Veronica Guerin would discuss a matter in which on that premise they had an obvious interest.

Reference has been made to information contained in the original statement made by Ms Bacon, now Bowden's wife, which it is alleged casts some doubt on his account of his movements on the day of the murder. That statement is not evidence and it has emerged also that Ms Bacon made subsequent statements to the police which contradict some of the information originally given by her. The information in question, if it had been given by the latter on oath as a witness in the trial, does not establish the contention that the first lieutenant met Bowden and handed over the gun to him on the afternoon of the killing. For the reasons already referred to the Court is satisfied that no such hand-over took place.

Evidence has been led on behalf of the accused which purports to establish that after the killing, the first lieutenant and the gunman drove to a premises called RNT Engineering in an industrial estate off the Belgard Road.

There is some evidence to suggest that a motorbike with two crash-helmeted persons on it may have been ridden around to the back of the factory premises. If that were so then it would suggest that the motorcycle may have been hidden there and not brought to the accused's house in Walkinstown Road as alleged by the prosecution. The relevant witnesses were not *ad idem* and the evidence is not sufficiently clear to establish that proposition or to raise a reasonable doubt in the mind of the Court in that regard.

A matter to which much importance is given by the accused is that, being a drug addict, he would not have been recruited by the organisers of the crime to play any part in it – far less the crucial role of receiving and disposing of the motorcycle and the gun. That argument does not stand up to critical analysis and the Court notes in particular the following facts:-

(i) If the accused's capacity and reliability was significantly impaired by heroin abuse which was on-going for a period of weeks at the material time as he alleges, his criminal business associates would not have allowed him to continue performing his pivotal role of collecting very large sums of money from wholesale customers on a daily basis. If in that state he could readily have jeopardised the whole operation.

(ii) The accused's contention as to incapacity flies in the face of the case which he makes that he had sufficient iron discipline to maintain total silence during a series of major interrogations by police officers over the 48 hour period of his Section 30 detention.

(iii) On his evidence his own mother was not aware of his addiction. She is the matriarch of the Ward family and would have had no difficulty in discerning the sort of symptoms described by the accused and Ms Meehan.

(iv) The accused's performance at the Green Isle Hotel in aid of his brother Shay is not that of a person significantly affected by drugs.

(v) Likewise, the accused's commendable conduct in providing refuge and treatment for his niece, Natasha, who was then grievously afflicted by heroin abuse is not the conduct of a person who is himself a serious drug-addict.

(vi) The accused did not appear to Dr Williams as having a significant drug-addiction problem.

(vii) There is no medical evidence adduced in support of the accused's contention.

The Court is satisfied that the accused did not have a significant personal drug problem when arrested in October or in June 1996. It is probable that the physeptone was sought by him while in custody as a prop to help in sustaining the case which the accused subsequently made that he was a serious drug-addict and, therefore, incapable of participating in the murder of Ms Guerin as alleged.

Finally, the Court has been urged to disregard the telephone evidence which has been given. At best from the prosecution point of view it establishes no more than that on the day of the murder a large number of very short telephone calls passed between mobile phones owned by respectively the accused and the first lieutenant and also related landline calls. Some of these occurred very close to the time when Ms. Guerin was murdered. There is, of course no evidence as to who made the calls or what was said. As Mr Leahy and Mr Charlton have fairly conceded they are not corroborative of the prosecution case but may be supportive of it. That seems to be a fair description of the relevance such as it may be.

In conclusion, having reviewed the relevant evidence in this trial with meticulous care, in particular that of Charles Bowden and the accused, the Court is satisfied beyond reasonable doubt that the accused, Paul Ward, was an accessory before the fact to the murder of Ms Veronica Guerin on 26th June, 1996 and therefore is guilty of the offence charged in the indictment."

I had moved down to the floor of the court beside the legal benches about three quarters way through the judgment. I hoped to see the expression on the face of the accused after the last line had been read out. I wanted to know if the man was capable of emotion one way or another. Mr Justice Barr stopped reading at 12.35pm. Paul Ward's impassive gaze lasted 30 seconds before tears welled up in his eyes and his mouth quivered. As he was being led away, he gestured to Vanessa Meehan that he would phone her. Within minutes, the court was empty.

You were vindicated, Veronica, the truth and justice you lived and died for had been done and seen to be done.

One day some weeks later I was writing at the newsdesk which you often occupied when talking to news editor Willie Kealy. I rose at one stage to stretch my legs and turning to the table behind I came across a dust-covered black book with the title *Book of Condolences.* As I moved some papers back another 100 books were revealed. They all contained the names and messages from the ordinary people of Ireland, the outpouring of grief from a nation bathed in tears. A note addressed to your memory fell from one of the books. A woman told of going to the *Stations of the Cross.* At one the priest said, "Veronica wiped the face of Jesus. This was no ordinary woman, she went through the crowd of onlookers and she wiped the face of Jesus in her towel". The woman concluded that your bravery matched hers, and as she was, you will be forever remembered. As the imprint of the face of Christ remained on her towel, so will yours on the consciousness of a country forever in your debt.

Work on the film progresses. Director John McKenzie, famous for his excellent British crime thriller *The Long Good Friday* has come on board and we met and hit it off. He is a witty Scotsman and entirely at home with our wild Celtic spirit. He initiates improvements to the script and his fresh eye eliminates some obvious weaknesses which we had missed. I continue at the centre of the creative work as I promised everyone I would when I vacated the director's chair. John brings in a writing partner Guy Edwards to do a final script polish. I go to London to meet him and we talk for three hours. He is intelligent and highly professional and I feel we are all singing from the same hymn sheet. *Irish Screen* have done well on the financing front with offers from *B Sky B*, French TV Station *Canal Plus*. I have only a cursory understanding of film finance but it seems like the film is going to get made in January 1999. Later on, after a lot of dithering, we received much needed finance from Bord Scannáin na hEireann (The Irish Film Board). Line producer John McDonnell rents production offices and when he tells me the location I suffer spiritual whiplash. How many times in this letter have I walked you down Northbrook Road? So many times I walked down the same road to meet you in Café Java and it took on a spiritual resonance after you crossed the river

261

into the trees. On this very road in the building which once housed St. Anne's Hospital in the shade of the cherry-blossom is the headquarters of the film-production unit. From a window I look down on the trees and already in mind's eye I see the buds blushing and slowly revealing their brilliant pink petals to the world.

One Month Later

We are in what is called in film parlance, pre-production, the preparation period before the actual shoot. The old wards of the former cancer hospital are occupied by location, wardrobe, production design and props people, working away under the eagle eye of line producer John McDonnell. Although I have read numerous books about the background life of a film the reality is only really grasped in the middle of it. John and Nigel and Michael Wearing have assembled what I am told is the Manchester United of Irish crews. Seamus Deasy acclaimed for his lighting on John Boorman's *The General* is Director of Photography with the legendary Des Whelan operating the camera. John MacKenzie has wisely decided that the job of lighting and operating will be too exhausting for one man on this project which will require six weeks on the streets of Dublin and two in a new studio complex in the north west of the city. The production designer who dictates the overall look and style of the film is Mark Geraghty whose most recent work was the luminous and visually delightful Dancing at Lughnasa. In my mind and John Mackenzie's vision we want to show the bright, cosmopolitan characterisations of Dublin as well as the dark, seamier side.

Mark co-ordinates with the locations department to choose the buildings, streets and backdrop that will best reflect the scope of the story. In one scene I have re-created a story you had told me about a meeting with an IRA commander who provided a taped interview of his interrogation of a major Dublin criminal who admitted his involvement in drug dealing. John and Mark have opted to locate this in the spectacular Baily lighthouse in Howth against the panoramic seascape of Dublin Bay. And this has a family connection. My partner, Ger's grandfather was the lighthouse keeper and her mother and her uncles were brought up in the lighthouse. I have placed your picture on the wall of every department, not that anyone needs any reminder of the significance of the project but it just feals appropriate and comforting to have you watching on during the eight weeks of preparation.

The shoot started on April 12, 1999 the same day as Cian's first birthday (he celebrated the day before). As the camera rolled over on a scene between the journalist (Joan Allen) and her main police contact (Patrick Bergin), I felt the tears welling up in my eyes. There were to be many more emotional scenes over the shoot, not only experienced by me but also by the cast and crew. Everything went exceedingly well unusual by normal standards but it felt like we were all on a mission. We didn't feel under any threat, but there were two armed detectives on the set every day. Twice your friend the Monk was spotted near two locations in Howth and Summerhill. There was nothing sinister, his visits I'm sure prompted by curiosity.

On June 2, 1999 two days before the shoot was due to

finish the trial of Brian Meehan began in the Special Criminal Court. Over the next seven weeks there were some extraordinary moments in the dramatic surroundings of Green Street. The recording of your last words to a Garda contact interrupted by the crackling sound of the first gunshots sent a chill around the courthouse. I relived those moments like those of previous terror you recalled to me in the Cafe Java. There was another recording of a conversation between the accused and Juliet Bacon, now wife of the supergrass Charles Bowden. Meehan's expletive filled threats of what would happen went to the core of his character. A dangerous criminal who would stop at nothing to keep his gang leader happy including offering to pull the trigger. His offer was declined because Meehan had failed in two attempts to assassinate gangland rival Martin Foley.

Meehan watched the proceedings with a mixture of indifference, contempt and nervous impatience. Only when his former gang members appeared in the witness box to give evidence or reporters looked at him to gauge reaction did his eyes dilate to pins and the workings of his ruthless mind translate to his face. He is small in stature and looks quite insignificant, but as all criminal gangs know, the little ones are the most dangerous.

The man who drove the motorbike on the day of the assassination and remarked to another member that the killer on the back had done a good job did not show a single trace of discomfort or remorse when the gory details of the act were recalled. Even his accomplice Russell Warren admitted to feeling sick after he had witnessed the killing, and another, Bowden, was haunted by visions in the aftermath.

But the Jack Russell of the gang folded his arms, looked up at the ceiling or to his father and mother in the public gallery, or into the body of the court. Nothing fazed Meehan, who had calmly pleaded not guilty to all 18 charges. Not even on the day of reckoning (Thursday July 29, 1999) did he show any sign of nervousness about the outcome – in contrast to the strained faces of the investigating officers, reporters and family. As presiding Judge Frederick Morris reached the point in his judgement where three key witnesses' evidence had been discredited, Meehan's prematurely greying head turned towards the gallery and he winked at his parents.

When the guillotine began to drop as Justice Morris declared that the court accepted Russell Warren's evidence, Meehan gaily handed out polo mints to his guards. As the guilty verdicts rained from the Bench, he sat and drummed his hands on his knees. When asked by court clerk Paddy Morrissey to stand for sentence, he adopted the same bantam cock stance and folded his tattooed arms across his chest in a clearly defiant gesture. He showed as much emotion as if the judge was reading out a shopping list. As he was being led down to the holding cell, he smiled at his weeping mother and told her he would ring her later.

There may not be one ounce of humanity or remorse in the mind of Brian Meehan but what is sure is that, where he is now, he will have plenty of time to contemplate - to think about his foul actions and what might have been. And if he ever sees the light of day, his hair will be a lot whiter and he will be about as old as his father is now.

Nobody could have summed it up better than Judge Frederick Morris. The last words of his judgement read:

"To those who grieve for the late Ms Guerin, the Court would like to say that by her death she contributed immeasurably to the successful identification and destruction of this drug importation and distribution enterprise. Hopefully this will have spared many young people from the scourge of drugs. If this is so, then her death will not have been in vain."

Your Friend and Colleague
Michael Sheridan
August 1999

A NOTE ON THE AUTHOR

For twenty years, Michael Sheridan combined a career as sports and arts journalist with that of theatre director. He scripted and directed *Lenny* - a one man show on the life of Lenny Bruce, which won top award at the Edinburgh Fringe Festival. He has a portfolio of forty professional productions to his credit.

As film correspondent for the *Sunday Independent* he interviewed many of the top names in Hollywood.

He was one of the first in Ireland to undertake a full-length triathlon to raise funds for cancer research and he was co-founder of The Annual Women's Mini-Marathon which is the most successful women's fun run in the world.